The New Mixer's Guide to

Low-Alcohol & Nonalcoholic Drinks

The New Mixer's Guide to

Low-Alcohol & Nonalcoholic Drinks

Sheila Buff and
Judi Olstein

HPBooks

ANOTHER BEST-SELLING VOLUME FROM HPBooks®
Publisher: Rick Bailey
Editorial Director: Elaine R. Woodard
Editor: Rebecca LaBrum

HPBooks

Published by HPBooks, Inc.
P.O. Box 5367, Tucson, AZ 85704 602/888-2150
ISBN 0-89586-458-4
Library of Congress Catalog Card Number 85-82369

This book was designed and produced by
Footnote Productions Ltd.
6 Blundell Street
London N7 9BH, England

Composition by Central Southern Typesetters, Eastbourne, E. Sussex, U.K.
Color origination by Hong Kong Scanner Craft Co. Ltd., Hong Kong
Printed by Regent Publishing Services Ltd., Hong Kong

1st Printing

Contents

SPALDING
SPALDING
SPALDING

Less Alcohol, More Fun

America's drinking habits are undergoing a rapid and important change: hard liquor is being replaced by low-alcohol and nonalcoholic beverages. Inspired in equal parts by the new concern for physical fitness and by growing nationwide concern about drunk driving, many people today choose mineral water over martinis.

The new wave in drinking means a new wave in entertaining. No longer does giving a party mean refilling the liquor cabinet. More likely, it means stocking up on wine, fruit juice, sparkling water—even cocoa powder—to make the drinks many guests now request.

Entertaining without alcohol is easy. As the hundreds of recipes in this book show, there's a vast range of low-alcohol and nonalcoholic drinks. Hot weather or cold, backyard barbecue or elegant dinner party, intimate gathering or open house, you'll find beverages for every occasion and every taste. Most are easily and quickly made with no special ingredients or equipment; in addition, most are quite inexpensive. But best of all, these drinks taste good. Your guests will never miss the alcohol.

Not only is alcohol high in calories, it actually robs the body of nutrition. It's no wonder that as more and more people decide to shape up and watch their diets, fewer and fewer drink alcoholic beverages. But by giving up alcohol, you don't give up any pleasure. The relaxing effect of a refreshing, sophisticated drink can still be enjoyed through the recipes in this volume.

People trying to cut back on alcohol consumption sometimes assume that a glass of wine or beer contains less alcohol than a cocktail. This is a common and potentially dangerous mistake. Twelve ounces of beer, 5 ounces of wine and 1¼ ounces of hard liquor—the standard serving portions—all have the same amount of alcohol. Their liquid volumes differ, but all three are equivalent in alcoholic content.

Less alcohol means more fun. Food tastes better when the tongue isn't numbed by liquor. Conversation is more intelligent. And for the hosts, there's the comforting knowledge that when guests leave, they can drive home safely.

Today's concerned hosts know that it is now perfectly acceptable not to serve alcoholic drinks when they entertain. Those who do serve alcohol are increasingly aware that some guests will choose not to drink it. In either case, this book will help you offer your guests a choice.

KRUPS
CAFFÈ
VAPORE

The Basics

Successful entertaining without alcohol is easy and enjoyable, especially if you follow these guidelines.

Ingredients. Always use the freshest and best possible ingredients when making a drink. You'll notice the difference. For example, although orange juice made from frozen concentrate tastes fine in a drink, freshly squeezed orange juice tastes even better.

Quantities. In any drink, proportion is important. A well-made drink has a good balance of flavors. Changing the quantity of a drink—by doubling or halving the recipe, for example—tends to affect its taste. If a recipe makes one serving and you'd like to serve two, make the drink twice rather than doubling the recipe.

Ice. Ice is crucial to successful entertaining (unless you're serving exclusively hot drinks, of course). Be sure to have plenty of it—running out of ice is the very worst thing that can happen when you entertain. Begin making ice in your freezer several days before the event, using fresh, clear water. Empty the ice cubes into large plastic bags, close them tightly and store in the freezer. During the party, remove the ice only as needed, so it stays hard and dry. Your ice bucket should never be full of half-melted ice cubes and water. When the party is over, discard any unused ice. Don't be tempted to keep it until the next time you entertain—ice that's stored too long will get a stale taste or pick up odors.

If you're planning to serve only one type of drink—iced tea, for example—prepare some in advance and fill your ice trays with it. Your guests will appreciate ice cubes that don't dilute their drinks as they melt.

To make cracked ice, wrap several ice cubes at a time in a clean kitchen towel. Hit the package decisively a few times with a hammer or mallet to break each ice cube into several pieces. To make crushed ice, follow the same procedure, but continue to hit the ice until each cube is broken into small pieces. Because it will melt quickly, prepare cracked or crushed ice only as you need it, not in advance.

Beverages. If the first rule for parties is never run out of ice, the second is never run out of things to drink. Be sure to stock up on carbonated beverages, wine and juice in advance of entertaining. Unopened bottles and cans of juice and carbonated beverages will keep almost indefinitely; unopened bottles of wine, if properly stored, will also keep well. Frozen juices can be stored for a long time, but fresh juice will usually start to lose its taste after a week or so in the refrigerator. In general, it is far, far better to have too much to drink than too little—buy more than you think you need and save the leftovers for the next party.

If you're serving a cold beverage made in quantity, you'll probably need to prepare it ahead, then chill it. But many drinks, especially those mixed in one- or two-serving amounts, should be served immediately after they're made. Always check the recipes you're using carefully—well in advance of the party.

GLASSWARE

Somehow, serving a drink in an attractive, sparkling-clean glass makes it taste better. Choose thin-lipped, clear glasses. Cut glass is fine, but try to avoid textures and colors—part of the enjoyment of a drink comes from seeing it in the glass. Since glasses unavoidably get broken, buy them from open stock so they can easily be replaced. Discard any glasses that are chipped or cracked.

Though it's possible to collect a whole cupboard full of specialized glasses, it isn't really necessary. You can get by quite nicely with just these glasses:

Wine glass. If you have some 10- to 14-ounce (1¼- to 1¾ cups) stemmed wine glasses, you need nothing else to entertain in style. Any cold drink is more elegant when served in a wine glass.

Highball glass. After the wine glass, the highball glass is the most useful all-purpose glass. Most have straight sides and hold from 8 to 12 ounces (1 to 1½ cups).

IN THIS BOOK, THE SUGGESTED GLASS FOR EACH DRINK IS PICTURED IN THE RECIPE.

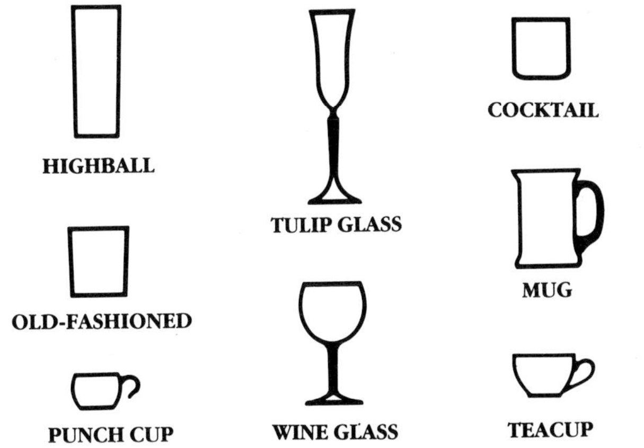

Old-fashioned glass. Also called a rocks or short glass, the old-fashioned glass holds between 8 and 10 ounces (1 and 1¼ cups).

Mug. For informal occasions, 8- to 10-ounce (1- to 1¼-cups) heatproof mugs, either glass or ceramic, are ideal for hot drinks. In more formal settings—at an elegant dinner party, for example—it's best to serve hot beverages in teacups and saucers.

Punch cups. A punch cup generally has a handle and holds 6 to 8 ounces (¾ to 1 cup). Punch cups are usually sold in sets with the punch bowl, so they can be difficult to replace if broken.

Disposables. Glasses made of clear plastic are widely available in a number of sizes and shapes. Inexpensive and disposable, they can make entertaining, particularly when the party is large, much easier and more enjoyable. For hot drinks, foam cups are a better choice than paper cups with handles.

EQUIPMENT

Making delicious low-alcohol and nonalcoholic drinks requires very little special equipment—the average kitchen probably already holds everything you need.

Blender. Called for in many recipes, a blender is the best way to give many drinks a smooth, creamy texture.

Other tools and equipment. Measuring cups and spoons are essential; other useful tools include a bottle/can opener, corkscrew, whisk, hand beater, sieve and citrus juicer. You'll also find bottle caps, an ice-cream scoop, a citrus zester and nutmeg grater helpful to have on hand. A small, sharp knife and a cutting board make slicing and chopping easier. A supply of cheesecloth comes in handy for making drinks that must be strained before serving.

Coasters are good protection for your furniture; set them out at party time to prevent drink glasses from making rings on wood surfaces. It's also a good idea to serve drinks with small napkins.

Ice tools. Use ice trays that produce a medium cube; very small cubes melt too quickly and dilute the drink. Keep a hammer handy for making cracked and crushed ice. Ice buckets are useful when drinks are made outside the kitchen. Cut glass ice containers are attractive, but they won't keep ice frozen for too long—be sure to use the ice quickly, before it melts. Ice keeps longer in insulated or foam ice buckets with lids, but these tend to take up a lot of space.

Tools for hot drinks. Tea infusers and a good coffeepot are indispensable. If you serve coffee and tea often, you'll probably want a few other tools as well; see pages 58 and 76. A double boiler for hot chocolate drinks is a good idea—and it has many other kitchen uses.

Bar tools. Cocktail shakers, coil-rimmed strainers, bar measures, bar spoons, sparkling water siphons and so on are used even for low-alcohol and nonalcoholic drinks.

SYRUPS

Most carbonated beverages are made simply from a mixture of syrup and sparkling water. You can buy flavored syrups if you wish, but why not make your own? Almost any fruit juice can be made into a syrup by cooking it with sugar. As a general rule, you will need 2 cups of sugar for every cup of juice. Combine the ingredients in a stainless-steel or enameled saucepan and boil over medium heat, stirring gently, until the syrup is thickened. Remove from heat, cool, pour into a clean container and store in the refrigerator. Unopened syrups will generally keep for about a month; after opening the container, use the syrup within 2 weeks. To serve, half-fill a glass with crushed ice. Add syrup to taste, then fill the glass with cold sparkling water.

GINGER SYRUP

1 cup finely chopped fresh gingerroot
2 cups water
1 ¼ cups sugar

Combine gingerroot and water in a medium stainless-steel or enameled saucepan. Bring to a boil; then reduce heat and simmer 5 minutes. Remove from heat, cover and let stand 12 to 24 hours. Strain mixture through cheesecloth into another saucepan; squeeze pulp to extract all liquid. Add sugar and bring to a boil over medium heat, stirring. Boil 5 minutes, skimming off froth. Remove from heat and cool completely. Strain into a clean container, cover and refrigerate. Makes 2 cups.

CHOCOLATE SYRUP

¾ cup unsweetened cocoa powder
1½ cups sugar
⅛ teaspoon salt
1 cup hot water
2 teaspoons pure vanilla extract

Combine cocoa, sugar and salt in a medium saucepan. Gradually stir in water until mixture is smooth. Bring to a boil over medium heat, stirring; boil, stirring, 3 minutes. Remove from heat and stir in vanilla. Cool syrup, then pour into a clean container, cover and refrigerate. Makes 2 cups.

BLUEBERRY SYRUP

2 cups fresh blueberries
½ cup sugar
1½ teaspoons grated lemon peel
¼ cup water

Combine blueberries, sugar, lemon peel and water in a medium stainless-steel or enameled saucepan. Heat over low heat, stirring, until sugar is dissolved. Bring to a boil, then reduce heat and simmer 8 minutes. Remove from heat and cool to lukewarm. Strain into a clean container, cover and refrigerate. Use within 2 weeks. Makes 2 cups.

GARNISHES

An ordinary drink takes on extra sparkle when served in an attractive glass with an interesting garnish. When choosing the garnish, keep both flavor and visual appeal in mind. Base the garnish on an ingredient in the drink—for example, you might garnish a glass of limeade with a lime slice. Or try something different and use a complementary garnish. For limeade, a slice of any other citrus fruit or a pineapple spear would be a good choice. If a drink has several main ingredients, select a garnish that highlights one of them.

You don't have to stop at just one garnish for a drink, of course. Use several if you want—try that glass of limeade with a lime slice *and* a mint sprig *and* a maraschino cherry. Just make sure there's always more drink than garnish.

If the garnish is a simple lemon wedge or mint sprig, simply drop it into the drink or hook it over the rim of the glass. If the garnish is more elaborate and is clearly meant to be eaten—a pineapple wedge with a maraschino cherry, for example—spear the ingredients together on an attractive pick. And remember that tall cold drinks are more fun when sipped through a colorful straw.

Preparing garnishes. No matter what the garnish is, be sure it's fresh. Try to prepare the garnish as it is needed or only shortly in advance. To cut slices of fruit, use a sharp knife on a cutting board. Peels can be left on, but remove any seeds and other inedible parts from the garnish. When using canned fruits, drain them well. If the garnish is to hang on the rim of the glass, cut a slit in it.

Citrus peel (or "zest") is often used as a garnish because the oils in the peel add a subtle aroma to the drink. You can cut strips of citrus peel with a vegetable peeler or a sharp knife, but the best tool for the job is an inexpensive gadget called a zester. This little device makes it extra-easy to remove strips of peel with no white pith attached.

Juices

Naturally delicious and high in nutrients, fruit and vegetable juices are delightfully refreshing beverages. Many juices are readily available in bottles, cartons, cans and frozen concentrates. The liquids are often reconstituted from frozen concentrate, however; they're also often diluted and sweetened with sugar. Frozen concentrates often contain added sugar as well. For the best flavor and greatest nutritional value, make your own juices.

Citrus juice. A citrus fruit will give more juice if you first roll it on a counter with the palm of your hand or warm it in a microwave oven for a few seconds. Cut the fruit in half crosswise and press the halves against the dome of a citrus juicer to force out the liquid. Watch out for seeds.

Soft fruits. Melons, berries, grapes, cherries and so forth can easily be made into juice. Start with very ripe fruit at room temperature. Rinse it well and remove any blemishes, stems and seeds. Cut the fruit into small pieces, place in a blender and process until pureed. Pour the puree into a large bowl, cover and refrigerate for several hours. Then strain the puree through a layer of cheesecloth into a pitcher.

Hard fruits and vegetables. To make juice from hard fruits and vegetables, rinse them well and remove any blemishes, stems and seeds. Chop coarsely, place in a saucepan, add enough water to cover and simmer until soft. Remove from heat and cool; then follow the instructions above for soft fruits.

The easy way. Electric juice extractors for citrus fruits are easy to use and fairly inexpensive. You can also buy machines that will press juice from any fruit or vegetable—oranges, peaches, tomatoes, you name it. These too are easy to use and give excellent results.

Many blenders and food processors have optional juicing attachments; using these, you can make delicious juice from fruits and vegetables with very little effort.

Serving. Chill all juices thoroughly before serving. Add a tiny pinch of salt to bring out the flavor of vegetable juices; sweeten fruit juices to taste with sugar or honey, if desired. Ice in the glass is optional. Store juices in the refrigerator, tightly covered; they'll keep for about a week.

ORANGEADE

¼ cup honey
4 cups water
2 cups orange juice
¼ cup lemon juice
1 orange, thinly sliced
Ice cubes

Dissolve honey in water in a large pitcher. Add orange juice, lemon juice and orange slices. Fill pitcher with ice cubes; stir. Makes 1½ quarts.

ORANGE FLIP

1 cup half and half
½ cup milk
1 egg
3 tablespoons sugar
¾ cup orange juice
¼ teaspoon freshly grated nutmeg

Combine half and half, milk, egg and sugar in a blender. Process on lowest speed 10 seconds. With motor still running, slowly add orange juice and nutmeg. Refrigerate until well chilled. Makes 2 servings.

SANGRITA (MEXICAN ORANGE JUICE)

5 cups orange juice
¾ cup Grenadine syrup
2½ teaspoons red (cayenne) pepper
½ teaspoon salt

Combine orange juice, Grenadine syrup, red pepper and salt in a pitcher. Stir well. Refrigerate until well chilled. Makes 1½ quarts.

LEFT TO RIGHT: ORANGE FLIP, TANGERINE SPECIAL, SANGRITA, SPARKLING ORANGEADE, ORANGEADE

SPARKLING ORANGEADE

1 cup sugar

2 cups water

$4\frac{1}{2}$ cups orange juice

$\frac{1}{2}$ cup lemon juice

2 oranges, thinly sliced

2 qts. cold sparkling water (8 cups)

Dissolve sugar in water in a large pitcher. Stir in orange juice, lemon juice and orange slices. Refrigerate until very cold. Fill pitcher with sparkling water; stir. Makes $3\frac{1}{2}$ quarts.

DUTCH ORANGE DRINK

1 pint milk (2 cups)

2 tablespoons whipping cream

1 cup orange juice

1 tablespoon lemon juice

3 tablespoons sugar

Ice cubes

Combine milk, cream, orange juice, lemon juice and sugar in a blender. Process 2 minutes. Serve over ice cubes. Makes 4 servings.

TANGERINE SPECIAL

2 tangerines, peeled, sectioned and seeded

1 lemon, peeled, sectioned and seeded

6 ice cubes

1 tablespoon sugar

2 cups water

Combine tangerine sections, lemon sections, ice cubes, sugar and water in a blender. Process on highest speed 10 seconds. Makes 4 servings.

BUTTERMILK LEMONADE

2 tablespoons sugar
¼ cup lemon juice
1 qt. buttermilk (4 cups)

Combine sugar and lemon juice in a pitcher; stir until sugar is dissolved. Stir in buttermilk. Refrigerate until well chilled. Makes 1 quart.

LEMON FROSTED

6 scoops lemon sherbet
4 cups chilled lemonade
Mint sprigs

For each serving, put 1 scoop sherbet into glass. Fill glass with lemonade. Garnish with mint sprigs. Makes 6 servings.

PINK LEMONADE

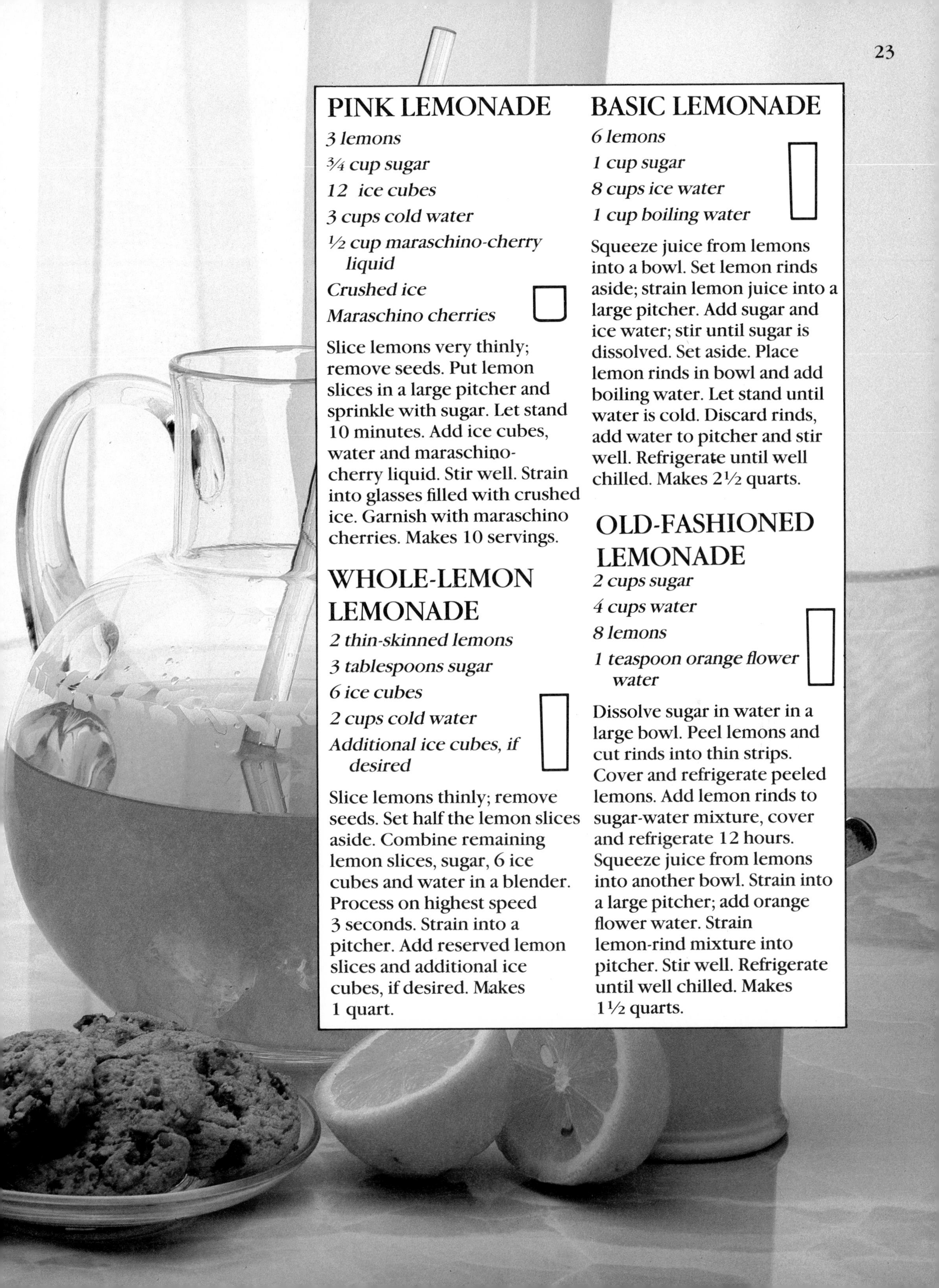

PINK LEMONADE

3 lemons
¾ cup sugar
12 ice cubes
3 cups cold water
½ cup maraschino-cherry liquid
Crushed ice
Maraschino cherries

Slice lemons very thinly; remove seeds. Put lemon slices in a large pitcher and sprinkle with sugar. Let stand 10 minutes. Add ice cubes, water and maraschino-cherry liquid. Stir well. Strain into glasses filled with crushed ice. Garnish with maraschino cherries. Makes 10 servings.

WHOLE-LEMON LEMONADE

2 thin-skinned lemons
3 tablespoons sugar
6 ice cubes
2 cups cold water
Additional ice cubes, if desired

Slice lemons thinly; remove seeds. Set half the lemon slices aside. Combine remaining lemon slices, sugar, 6 ice cubes and water in a blender. Process on highest speed 3 seconds. Strain into a pitcher. Add reserved lemon slices and additional ice cubes, if desired. Makes 1 quart.

BASIC LEMONADE

6 lemons
1 cup sugar
8 cups ice water
1 cup boiling water

Squeeze juice from lemons into a bowl. Set lemon rinds aside; strain lemon juice into a large pitcher. Add sugar and ice water; stir until sugar is dissolved. Set aside. Place lemon rinds in bowl and add boiling water. Let stand until water is cold. Discard rinds, add water to pitcher and stir well. Refrigerate until well chilled. Makes 2½ quarts.

OLD-FASHIONED LEMONADE

2 cups sugar
4 cups water
8 lemons
1 teaspoon orange flower water

Dissolve sugar in water in a large bowl. Peel lemons and cut rinds into thin strips. Cover and refrigerate peeled lemons. Add lemon rinds to sugar-water mixture, cover and refrigerate 12 hours. Squeeze juice from lemons into another bowl. Strain into a large pitcher; add orange flower water. Strain lemon-rind mixture into pitcher. Stir well. Refrigerate until well chilled. Makes 1½ quarts.

LIMEADE

4 tablespoons honey

5 cups water

1 cup lime juice

Combine honey and 1 cup water in a saucepan. Bring to a boil, then reduce heat and simmer 6 minutes. Pour mixture into a pitcher; add remaining 4 cups water and lime juice and stir well. Refrigerate until well chilled. Makes 1½ quarts.

SPARKLING LIMEADE

1 lime, sliced

Whole cloves

1 cup water

2 cups lime juice

1 qt. cold sparkling water (4 cups)

½ cup sugar

Crushed ice

Stud lime slices with cloves and set aside. Combine water, lime juice and sparkling water in a large pitcher. Add sugar and stir until dissolved. Serve in glasses half-filled with crushed ice. Garnish with clove-studded lime slices. Makes 2 quarts.

PINEAPPLE-GRAPEFRUIT JUICE

⅓ cup sugar

⅓ cup water

1¼ cups unsweetened grapefruit juice

⅔ cup unsweetened pineapple juice

¼ cup lemon juice

Combine sugar and water in a small saucepan. Bring to a boil, then reduce heat and simmer 3 minutes. Remove from heat and cool. Pour into a small pitcher and add grapefruit juice, pineapple juice and lemon juice. Stir well. Refrigerate until well chilled. Makes 4 servings.

RASPBERRY-LIME SWIZZLE

2 cups frozen raspberries, thawed and drained
1½ cups sugar
8 cups cold water
1⅔ cups lime juice
Lime slices

Puree raspberries in a blender or a food processor fitted with a metal blade. Strain and set aside. Combine sugar, 2 cups water and ⅓ cup lime juice in a saucepan. Stir until sugar is dissolved. Bring to a boil, then reduce heat and simmer 6 minutes. Remove from heat, cool and pour into a large pitcher. Add raspberry puree, remaining 6 cups water and remaining 1⅓ cups lime juice. Stir well; refrigerate until well chilled. Garnish with lime slices. Makes 2½ quarts.

CUCUMBER-LEMON LIMEADE

2 cups sugar
8 cups water
1½ cups lemon juice
1 cup lime juice
1 cup thin cucumber slices
Mint sprigs

Combine sugar and 4 cups water in a large pitcher. Stir until sugar is dissolved. Add remaining 4 cups water, lemon juice, lime juice and cucumber slices. Stir well; refrigerate until well chilled. Garnish with mint sprigs. Makes 3 quarts.

GRAPEFRUIT-CARROT COCKTAIL

3 carrots, peeled and coarsely chopped
½ cup water
4 cups unsweetened grapefruit juice
1½ tablespoons Grenadine syrup
⅛ teaspoon ground ginger
1½ cups crushed ice

Put carrots in a small saucepan and add water. Cover and cook over low heat 10 minutes or until carrots are tender. Drain well, reserving ¼ cup cooking liquid. Puree carrots and reserved ¼ cup liquid in a blender. Add grapefruit juice, Grenadine syrup, ginger and crushed ice. Process until frothy. Serve at once. Makes 1¼ quarts.

LEFT TO RIGHT: SPARKLING LIMEADE, CUCUMBER-LEMON LIMEADE, GRAPEFRUIT-CARROT COCKTAIL, RASPBERRY-LIME SWIZZLE, LIMEADE

CITRUS MEDLEY

¾ cup unsweetened grapefruit juice
½ cup lemon juice
½ cup orange juice
⅓ cup sugar
1 cup crushed ice
Mint sprigs

Combine grapefruit juice, lemon juice, orange juice, sugar and crushed ice in a pitcher. Stir until well chilled. Garnish with mint sprigs. Makes 4 servings.

MANGO ORANGO

3 cups water
½ cup sugar
1 tablespoon grated orange peel
2 cups mashed mangoes
1 cup orange juice
½ cup lemon juice

Combine water, sugar and orange peel in a saucepan. Heat, stirring, until sugar is dissolved. Remove from heat and cool. Pour into a pitcher. Add mangoes, orange juice and lemon juice. Mix well. Refrigerate until well chilled. Makes 2 quarts.

PURPLE LEMON COOLER

½ cup prune juice
½ cup lemon juice
1 teaspoon powdered sugar
Ice cubes
Mint sprig

Combine prune juice, lemon juice and powdered sugar in glass. Stir well. Fill glass with ice cubes and garnish with mint sprig. Makes 1 serving.

ORANGE-CASHEW COOLER

½ cup coarsely chopped unsalted cashews
4 cups water
¼ cup honey
4 cups orange juice

Combine cashews, water, honey and orange juice in a blender. Process until smooth. Strain into a pitcher and refrigerate until well chilled. Makes 2 quarts.

LEFT TO RIGHT: MINTY CITRUS COMBO, ORANGE GINGERADE, ORANGE-CASHEW COOLER, CITRUS MEDLEY, MANGO ORANGO

MINTY CITRUS COMBO

½ cup unsweetened grapefruit juice
½ cup orange juice
1 tablespoon lime juice
2 mint sprigs
Ice cubes

Combine grapefruit juice, orange juice, lime juice and 1 mint sprig in a blender. Process 5 seconds. Serve over ice cubes. Garnish with remaining mint sprig. Makes 1 serving.

ORANGE GINGERADE

½ lb. crystallized ginger, finely chopped
2 cups water
1½ cups sugar
1 cup unsweetened grapefruit juice
3 cups orange juice
Crushed ice

Combine ginger, water and sugar in a saucepan. Heat, stirring, until sugar is dissolved. Remove from heat, add grapefruit juice and orange juice and stir well. Cool, then strain into a pitcher. Fill pitcher with crushed ice. Makes 2 quarts.

MINT JEWEL

1 cup mint sprigs
½ cup lemon juice
1½ teaspoons grated lemon peel
2 cups water
¾ cup honey
½ cup orange juice
½ cup unsweetened pineapple juice

Crush mint sprigs in a large bowl. Add lemon juice and lemon peel; let stand 30 minutes. Combine water and honey in a saucepan; simmer 7 minutes, then pour over mint mixture. Add orange juice and pineapple juice. Stir well, strain into a pitcher and cool. Refrigerate until well chilled. Makes 1½ quarts.

MULLED APPLE CIDER

WASSAIL

6 (2- to 3-inch) cinnamon sticks

16 whole cloves

6 whole allspice berries

6 cups apple cider

2 cups cranberry juice

¼ cup sugar

1 teaspoon bitters

Tie cinnamon sticks, cloves and allspice together in a piece of cheesecloth. Combine cider, cranberry juice, sugar and bitters in a large saucepan. Add spice bag and simmer 10 minutes. Remove spice bag and serve hot. Makes 8 servings.

YULETIME CIDER

¼ cup half and half

1 egg

½ teaspoon powdered sugar

½ cup crushed ice

¾ cup apple cider

Freshly grated nutmeg

Combine half and half, egg and powdered sugar in a cocktail shaker with crushed ice. Shake vigorously and strain into glass. Add cider and sprinkle with nutmeg. Makes 1 serving.

APPLE TEA

1 apple, cored and thinly sliced

1 teaspoon grated lemon peel

1 cup boiling water

Sugar to taste

Put apple slices and lemon peel in a bowl; add water. Cool, then cover and refrigerate until cold. Strain into glass and sweeten with sugar. Makes 1 serving.

APPLE DULCET

1 (24-oz.) jar apple jelly

4 cups boiling water

8 cups apple cider

½ teaspoon freshly grated nutmeg

6 egg whites

⅓ cup powdered sugar

Mint sprigs

Beat together jelly and water in a very large bowl until frothy. Cool. Add cider and nutmeg. Refrigerate until well chilled. Place egg whites in a bowl and beat until soft peaks form. Gradually add powdered sugar, beating until whites are stiff but not dry. Pour cider mixture into glasses and top with meringue. Garnish with mint sprigs. Makes 8 servings.

MULLED CIDER

6 cups apple cider

3 tablespoons packed light-brown sugar

5 (2- to 3-inch) cinnamon sticks

6 whole allspice berries

8 whole cloves

¼ teaspoon freshly grated nutmeg

Combine cider, brown sugar, 1 cinnamon stick, allspice, cloves and nutmeg in a large stainless-steel or enameled saucepan. Bring to a boil; then reduce heat and simmer, stirring, 10 minutes. Remove from heat, cool, cover and refrigerate 12 hours or overnight. Reheat over medium heat and strain into mugs. Garnish each serving with 1 of the remaining cinnamon sticks. Makes 4 servings.

PINEAPPLE SNOW

3 tablespoons chopped fresh or canned pineapple

1 tablespoon lime juice

1 ½ teaspoons sugar

½ cup crushed ice

Lime slice

Combine pineapple, lime juice and sugar in a blender. Process 5 seconds on highest speed. Place crushed ice in glass; pour pineapple mixture over ice. Garnish with lime slice. Makes 1 serving.

GARAPIÑA (CARIBBEAN PINEAPPLE DRINK)

Peel of 1 pineapple, coarsely chopped

2½ cups water

3 tablespoons sugar

Place pineapple peel in a pitcher. Add water, cover and let stand 24 hours in a warm place. Strain into another pitcher, stir in sugar and refrigerate until very well chilled. Makes 2½ cups.

SUNNY SIPPER

1 ½ cups unsweetened pineapple juice

1 orange, peeled, sectioned and seeded

1 medium carrot, peeled and cut into chunks

1 tablespoon golden seedless raisins

3 ice cubes

Combine pineapple juice, orange sections, carrot and raisins in a blender. Process 1 minute or until smooth. Add ice cubes and process 5 more seconds. Makes 1 serving.

MULLED PINEAPPLE JUICE

6 cups unsweetened pineapple juice

1 (2- to 3-inch) cinnamon stick

4 whole cloves

2 tablespoons honey

Combine pineapple juice, cinnamon stick and cloves in a medium saucepan. Bring to a boil; then reduce heat, cover and simmer 20 minutes. Remove cinnamon stick and cloves. Stir in honey. Serve hot. Makes 6 servings.

PINEAPPLE CUKIE

1 small cucumber, peeled, seeded and thinly sliced

1 cup unsweetened pineapple juice

½ cup watercress sprigs

4 parsley sprigs

½ cup crushed ice

Combine cucumber slices, pineapple juice, watercress, 2 parsley sprigs and crushed ice in a blender. Process 10 seconds or until smooth. Garnish with remaining 2 parsley sprigs. Makes 2 servings.

PINEAPPLE-BANANA COMBO

1½ cups unsweetened pineapple juice

1 banana, sliced

2 teaspoons honey

2 tablespoons lime juice

½ cup crushed ice

Mint sprigs

Combine pineapple juice, banana, honey, lime juice and crushed ice in a blender. Process 10 seconds or until smooth. Garnish with mint sprigs. Makes 2 servings.

LEFT TO RIGHT: MULLED PINEAPPLE JUICE, SUNNY SIPPER, PINEAPPLE CUKIE, GARAPIÑA

HOT CRANBERRY GROG

1 cup fresh or frozen cranberries

½ cup water

1 tablespoon honey

¾ cup unsweetened pineapple juice

6 whole allspice berries

8 whole cloves

¼ teaspoon freshly grated nutmeg

1 (2- to 3-inch) cinnamon stick

Combine cranberries, water, honey, pineapple juice, allspice, cloves, nutmeg and cinnamon stick in a medium saucepan. Bring to a boil; then reduce heat, cover and simmer 15 minutes. Strain into mugs and serve immediately. Makes 2 servings.

CRANBERRY FROTH

¾ cup cranberry juice

2 tablespoons raspberry jam

½ teaspoon lemon juice

3 ice cubes

Orange slice

Combine cranberry juice, jam, lemon juice and ice cubes in a blender. Process until frothy. Garnish with orange slice. Makes 1 serving.

RASPBERRY FIZZ

½ cup fresh or frozen raspberries, thawed if frozen

¼ cup orange juice

2 teaspoons lemon juice

1 tablespoon sugar

6 ice cubes

Cold sparkling water

Mint sprigs

Combine raspberries, orange juice, lemon juice and sugar in a blender. Process 10 seconds or until smooth. Add ice cubes and process 10 more seconds. Pour into glasses; fill glasses with sparkling water. Garnish with mint sprigs. Makes 4 servings.

RASPBERRY SHRUB

1 cup fresh or frozen raspberries, thawed if frozen

½ cup ice water

1 thin lemon slice, with rind

1 teaspoon honey

Mint sprig

Combine raspberries, ice water, lemon slice and honey in a blender. Process until smooth. Refrigerate until well chilled. Garnish with mint sprig. Makes 1 serving.

RASPBERRY GRANITA

¾ cup fresh or frozen raspberries, thawed if frozen

1 cup water

⅓ cup sugar

Whipped cream

Puree raspberries in a blender or a food processor fitted with a metal blade. Press puree through a sieve into a bowl. Add water and sugar; stir well. Pour mixture into ice trays or a shallow dish. Place in freezer about 1 hour or until frozen at edges but soft in center. Stir mixture well. Freeze 1 to 2 more hours. Empty mixture into a bowl and crush with a spatula to break up large ice crystals. Serve topped with whipped cream. Makes 4 servings.

CRANBERRY SPIKE

2 cups cranberry juice

1½ cups apricot nectar

2 tablespoons lemon juice

Ice cubes

Combine cranberry juice, apricot nectar and lemon juice in a 1-quart pitcher. Stir well; fill pitcher with ice cubes. Makes 1 quart.

LEFT TO RIGHT: RASPBERRY FIZZ, CRANBERRY FROTH

BERRY DRINKS

STRAWBERRY FROST

STRAWBERRY FROST

¾ cup fresh strawberries, hulled, or frozen strawberries

1 cup orange juice

2 tablespoons sugar

9 ice cubes

Combine strawberries, orange juice, sugar and ice cubes in a blender. Process 1 minute or until smooth. Makes 1 serving.

STRAWBERRY CUP

10 cups fresh strawberries, hulled

¼ cup cider vinegar

4 cups sugar

Crushed ice

Crush strawberries in a large glass or ceramic bowl. Add vinegar. Cover bowl and let stand 4 days in a cool place. Strain through a sieve lined with cheesecloth into a saucepan. Add sugar and bring to a boil, stirring until sugar is dissolved. Reduce heat and simmer 5 minutes. Remove from heat and cool. Serve in glasses filled with crushed ice. Makes 1 quart.

STRAWBERRY SQUIRT

6 fresh strawberries, hulled

8 oz. vanilla yogurt (1 cup)

¾ cup cold sparkling water

Combine strawberries and yogurt in a blender. Process on highest speed until smooth. Stir in sparkling water. Makes 2 servings.

BLUEBERRY FIZZ

3 tablespoons Blueberry Syrup, page 15 or purchased blueberry syrup

3 tablespoons cream of coconut

4 ice cubes

3 tablespoons fresh or frozen blueberries

Cold sparkling water

Lemon slice

Combine Blueberry Syrup and cream of coconut in glass. Stir well. Add ice cubes and blueberries. Fill glass with sparkling water and stir. Garnish with lemon slice. Makes 1 serving.

BLUEBERRY COOLER

¼ cup orange juice

½ teaspoon powdered sugar

4 ice cubes

Ginger ale

3 tablespoons fresh or frozen blueberries

Orange slice

Combine orange juice and powdered sugar in glass. Stir well. Add ice cubes and fill glass with ginger ale. Add blueberries. Garnish with orange slice. Makes 1 serving.

STRAWBERRY GRANITA

1 cup sugar

⅔ cup water

5 cups fresh strawberries, hulled

1 tablespoon lemon juice

¼ cup orange juice

4 fresh strawberries, hulled

Combine sugar and water in a small saucepan. Bring to a boil, stirring until sugar is dissolved. Reduce heat and simmer 5 minutes. Remove from heat, cool and set aside. Press 5 cups strawberries through a sieve into a bowl. Add lemon juice and orange juice. Stir in sugar-water mixture. Pour into ice trays or a shallow dish. Place in freezer about 1½ hours or until frozen at edges but soft in center. Stir mixture well. Freeze 2 more hours. Empty mixture into a bowl and crush with a spatula to break up large ice crystals. Serve in parfait or wine glasses; garnish each serving with a strawberry. Makes 4 servings.

APRICOT-JAM DRINK

2 cups apricot jam

2 cups water

1½ teaspoons grated lemon peel

3 tablespoons lemon juice

Ice cubes

Combine jam, water and lemon peel in a heavy stainless-steel or enameled saucepan. Bring to a boil; then reduce heat and simmer 2 minutes. Strain into a pitcher; add lemon juice. Cool. Serve over ice cubes. Makes 1 quart.

PEACH & OATMEAL DRINK

2½ cups water

3 tablespoons rolled oats

1 very ripe peach

2 tablespoons peach preserves

¼ cup orange juice

Combine water and oats in a small saucepan. Bring to a boil; then reduce heat and simmer 3 minutes. Remove from heat and cool. Peel, pit and slice peach; set aside. Process oat mixture in a blender until very smooth. Add peach, preserves and orange juice. Process until smooth. Makes 2 servings.

GRAPE COOLER

½ cup sugar

2 cups cold water

2 cups grape juice

1½ cups orange juice

¾ cup lemon juice

Combine sugar and water in a pitcher and stir until sugar is dissolved. Add grape juice, orange juice and lemon juice. Stir well. Refrigerate until well chilled. Makes 1½ quarts.

NECTARINE NECTAR

4 very ripe nectarines
½ cup orange juice
1 tablespoon lemon juice
1 tablespoon sugar
1 cup crushed ice

Peel, pit and slice nectarines. Combine nectarines, orange juice, lemon juice, sugar and crushed ice in a blender. Process 1 minute or until smooth. Serve at once. Makes 2½ cups.

GRAPE EYE-OPENER

2½ cups grape juice
½ cup plain yogurt
½ cup milk
2 egg yolks
1 banana, sliced
1 cup melon cubes

Combine grape juice, yogurt, milk, egg yolks, banana and melon in a blender. Process until smooth. Makes 4 servings.

MULLED APRICOT NECTAR

1 (46-oz.) can apricot nectar
½ lemon, sliced
2 (2- to 3-inch) cinnamon sticks
15 whole cloves
8 whole allspice berries

Combine apricot nectar, lemon slices, cinnamon sticks, cloves and allspice in a heavy saucepan. Bring to a boil; then reduce heat and simmer 5 minutes. Remove from heat, cover and cool 30 minutes. Reheat just until hot and strain into mugs. Makes 6 servings.

LEFT TO RIGHT: NECTARINE NECTAR, APRICOT-JAM DRINK, MULLED APRICOT NECTAR, GRAPE EYE-OPENER, GRAPE COOLER

WATERMELON WHIRL

4 cups cubed, seeded watermelon
½ cup apricot nectar
¼ cup lime juice
2 tablespoons honey
Lime slices

Puree watermelon in a blender. Add apricot nectar, lime juice and honey. Process 10 seconds. Garnish with lime slices. Makes 6 servings.

FOUR-FRUIT COMBO

1½ cups unsweetened pineapple juice
1 orange, peeled, sectioned and seeded
½ apple, peeled, cored and sliced
½ pear, peeled, cored and sliced
Ice cubes

Combine pineapple juice, orange sections, apple slices and pear slices in a blender. Process until smooth. Serve over ice cubes. Makes 4 servings.

CASHEW-FRUIT BLEND

2 cups orange juice
1 cup fresh strawberries, hulled
½ cup chopped unsalted cashews
2 cups honeydew cubes

Combine orange juice, strawberries, cashews and honeydew in a blender. Process until smooth. Serve immediately. Makes 6 servings.

PRUNEBERRY

Ice cubes

½ cup prune juice

½ cup cranberry juice

Mint sprig

Fill glass with ice cubes. Add prune juice and cranberry juice. Stir well. Garnish with mint sprig. Makes 1 serving.

PAYASAM (INDIAN SUMMER DRINK)

6 ripe mangoes

¼ cup cream of coconut

3 cups water

½ cup sugar

½ teaspoon ground cardamom

Ice cubes

¼ cup unsalted cashews, chopped

Peel and pit mangoes. Puree flesh in a blender; place in a large bowl. Add cream of coconut, water, sugar and cardamom. Mix well, then refrigerate until well chilled. Serve over ice cubes. Garnish with cashews. Makes 2 quarts.

CANTALOUPE-ORANGE BLEND

1 orange, peeled, sectioned and seeded

1 cup cantaloupe cubes

2 tablespoons lemon juice

⅛ teaspoon salt

½ cup crushed ice

Combine orange sections, cantaloupe, lemon juice, salt and crushed ice in a blender. Process until smooth. Makes 2 servings.

ENTER
HOME

TOMATO CREAM

1½ cups tomato juice
1 pint very cold milk (2 cups)
1 tablespoon lemon juice
1 teaspoon chopped onion
¼ teaspoon hot-pepper sauce

Combine tomato juice, milk, lemon juice, onion and hot-pepper sauce in a blender. Process until smooth. Serve immediately. Makes 4 servings.

TOMATO-CUCUMBER JUICE

1 small cucumber
2 cups tomato juice
2 tablespoons olive oil
1 tablespoon red-wine vinegar
½ teaspoon salt
Ice cubes

Peel, seed and grate cucumber. Combine with tomato juice, oil, vinegar and salt in a 1-quart pitcher. Stir well. Fill pitcher with ice cubes. Makes 1 quart.

MEXICALI

1 cup tomato juice
½ small green hot pepper, seeded
1 fresh cilantro (coriander) sprig
⅛ teaspoon dried leaf oregano
2 avocado slices

Combine tomato juice, hot pepper, cilantro sprig, oregano and avocado in a blender. Process 30 seconds. Makes 1 serving.

SPICED SWEET TOMATO JUICE

1 (46-oz.) can tomato juice
6 tablespoons packed brown sugar
6 whole cloves
2 (2- to 3-inch) cinnamon sticks
½ lemon, sliced

Combine tomato juice, brown sugar, cloves, cinnamon sticks and lemon slices in a heavy saucepan. Bring to a boil; then reduce heat and simmer 5 minutes. Strain into mugs. Makes 6 servings.

COOKED HOMEMADE TOMATO JUICE

3 lbs. ripe tomatoes, chopped
½ cup water
1 small onion, chopped
2 celery stalks, chopped
1 bay leaf
3 parsley sprigs
1 teaspoon salt
¼ teaspoon paprika
½ teaspoon sugar

Press tomatoes through a sieve into a large saucepan. Add water, onion, celery, bay leaf and parsley sprigs; simmer 30 minutes. Strain into a pitcher. Add salt, paprika and sugar. Stir well. Refrigerate until well chilled. Makes 1½ quarts.

TOMATO JUICE CREOLE

1 cup tomato juice
1 slice green bell pepper
¼ teaspoon lime juice
¼ teaspoon hot-pepper sauce
1 small garlic clove
Salt and black pepper to taste

Combine tomato juice, bell pepper, lime juice, hot-pepper sauce, garlic, salt and black pepper in a blender. Process 30 seconds. Makes 1 serving.

UNCOOKED HOMEMADE TOMATO JUICE

1½ lbs. ripe tomatoes, chopped
Salt and pepper to taste
3 tablespoons lemon juice
2 tablespoons chopped fresh parsley

Press tomatoes through a sieve into a pitcher. Add salt, pepper, lemon juice and parsley. Stir well. Refrigerate until well chilled. Makes 3 cups.

TOMATO-CLAM JUICE

2⅔ cups tomato juice
1⅓ cups bottled clam juice
1 tablespoon lemon juice

Combine tomato juice, clam juice and lemon juice in a pitcher. Stir well. Refrigerate until well chilled. Makes 1 quart.

LEFT TO RIGHT: TOMATO-CLAM JUICE, TOMATO CREAM, TOMATO-LIME QUENCHER

ORANGE-CARROT JUICE

2 cups chopped carrots

1 orange, peeled, sectioned and seeded

4 ice cubes

⅛ teaspoon salt

Place carrots, orange sections and ice cubes in a juicer or juicing attachment of a food processor. Process until smooth. Empty into a bowl and stir in salt. Makes 2 cups.

LEFT TO RIGHT: ORANGE-CARROT JUICE, VEGETABLE COCKTAIL, CUCUMBER FRAPPÉ

EMERALD BLEND

1/3 cup chopped fresh parsley
6 cups unsweetened pineapple juice
10 lettuce leaves, chopped
1/3 cup chopped celery leaves
1/3 cup watercress sprigs
Parsley sprigs

Combine chopped parsley, pineapple juice, lettuce, celery leaves and watercress in a blender. Process until smooth. Refrigerate until well chilled. Garnish with parsley sprigs. Makes 6 servings.

ZUCCHINI REFRESHER

2 tablespoons olive oil
1 small onion, thinly sliced
2 cups diced zucchini
1 medium potato, peeled and diced
2 small carrots, peeled and thinly sliced
1 teaspoon dried leaf tarragon
1 tablespoon chopped fresh dill or 1 teaspoon dried dill weed
2 cups chicken broth
About 1 cup cold milk

Heat oil in a large saucepan. Add onion, zucchini, potato and carrots. Cook, stirring, until vegetables begin to soften. Add tarragon, dill and broth and bring to a boil. Reduce heat, cover and simmer until vegetables are tender. Remove from heat; cool, pour into a blender and process until smooth. Pour into a pitcher and refrigerate until well chilled. Stir in 1 cup milk just before serving; add more milk if desired. Makes 6 servings.

VEGETABLE COCKTAIL

1/2 medium cucumber
1 1/2 cups tomato juice
2/3 cup chopped celery
1 tablespoon soy sauce
1 teaspoon chopped fresh mint or 1/2 teaspoon dried leaf mint
Salt and pepper to taste
About 1 1/2 cups water
Watercress sprigs

Peel, seed and chop cucumber. Combine cucumber, tomato juice, celery, soy sauce, mint, salt and pepper in a blender. Process until smooth. Pour into a pitcher and stir in 1 1/2 cups water; add more water if desired. Refrigerate until well chilled. Garnish with watercress sprigs. Makes 1 quart.

CUCUMBER-AVOCADO BLEND

1 medium avocado
1 large cucumber
1/2 cup chopped fresh parsley
3 tablespoons lemon juice
1 tablespoon olive oil
2 cups crushed ice

Pit, peel and chop avocado. Peel cucumber, reserving peel; seed and chop cucumber flesh. Combine avocado, chopped cucumber, parsley, lemon juice and oil in a blender. Process until smooth. Add crushed ice and process until smooth. Strain into glasses. Garnish with reserved cucumber peel. Makes 4 servings.

DILLED CUCUMBER DRINK

1 small cucumber
1 celery stalk, coarsely chopped
1 teaspoon chopped fresh dill or 1/2 teaspoon dried dill weed
1/2 teaspoon soy sauce
1 cup buttermilk

Peel, seed and chop cucumber. Combine cucumber, celery, dill, soy sauce and buttermilk in a blender. Process until smooth. Refrigerate until well chilled. Makes 1 serving.

CUCUMBER FRAPPÉ

3 large cucumbers
24 oz. plain yogurt (3 cups)
1/4 cup chopped fresh parsley
1/4 cup chopped fresh mint
9 ice cubes

Peel cucumbers, reserving peel of 1 cucumber; seed and chop cucumber flesh. Set aside. Combine yogurt, parsley and mint in a blender. Process until smooth. Add chopped cucumber, 1/3 at a time, and process until smooth. Add ice cubes and process until crushed. Garnish with reserved cucumber peel. Makes 6 servings.

Carbonated Drinks

The tiny bubbles that give fizz and tingle to carbonated drinks come from carbon dioxide—either contained in the liquid naturally or added to it artificially. Favorite carbonated beverages include sparkling water, soda pop and beer.

Sparkling water. If the label on the bottle says "naturally sparkling mineral water," the bubbles come from the same source as the water. If the label says "sparkling natural mineral water," the bubbles have been added; club soda or seltzer falls into this category. Despite advertising claims to the contrary, there is really little difference between naturally carbonated and carbonation-added sparkling waters. Few people can really tell the difference between an expensive imported brand and the cheapest supermarket brand. Your choice should be based simply on personal preference.

Soda pop. When sparkling water is combined with a flavored syrup, the result is soda pop. These vastly popular beverages are available in a wide choice of brands and flavors. You can also make your own soda pop from sparkling water and flavoring ingredients, as explained on pages 14 and 46.

Storage. Sparkling water and soda pop can be purchased well in advance and stored for months on end. They should be refrigerated for several hours before serving. Once the bottle has been opened, the carbonation will dissipate quickly and the beverage will become flat and tasteless. Cap opened bottles tightly and store them in the refrigerator; use the contents as quickly as possible.

Beer. Beers can be divided into four main groups, based on alcohol content: regular, light, low-alcohol and nonalcoholic. Because they contain less alcohol and fewer calories than regular and light beers, low-alcohol and nonalcoholic types are currently increasing in popularity.

Regular beer contains between 3.5 and 5 percent alcohol by weight; there are about 150 calories in a 12-ounce (1½-cup) serving. Light beer has about 3.1 percent alcohol and 100 calories per serving. Low-alcohol beer contains less than 2 percent alcohol; one serving supplies between 70 and 110 calories. All nonalcoholic beers have less than 0.5 percent alcohol. Calorie count per serving ranges from 50 to 85, depending on the type of beer: some are malt beverages that have never been fermented to form alcohol, while others are made from regular beer with the alcohol removed.

No matter what type of beer you choose, purchase it only shortly in advance. Even if unopened, beer loses its fresh flavor after about 3 months. Place beer in the refrigerator the day before serving; it tastes best at about 45°F (5°C). Pour and serve beer immediately after opening and discard any leftovers (or use in cooking)—open containers become flat and tasteless very quickly.

To pour beer, hold the glass at a 45-degree angle and pour the beer down the side of the glass until it's three-quarters full. Straighten the glass and fill it the rest of the way. The head of foam should be about ¾ inch thick.

HOMEMADE SODA POP

2 tablespoons flavored syrup; or 2 tablespoons frozen fruit juice concentrate, thawed; or ¾ cup cold fruit juice
Cold sparkling water
Ice cubes

Put syrup, concentrate or juice into glass. Add enough sparkling water to fill glass ¾ full. Stir gently. Add ice cubes. Makes 1 serving.

SUMMER SIPPER

Ice cubes
3 tablespoons lime juice
1½ teaspoons raspberry syrup
Cold sparkling water
Lime slice

Fill glass with ice cubes. Add lime juice and raspberry syrup. Fill glass with sparkling water and stir gently. Garnish with lime slice. Makes 1 serving.

CURRANT SPARKLER

1 tablespoon red currant jelly
2 tablespoons boiling water
Ice cubes
½ cup cold tonic water
Fresh strawberry, hulled
Lemon slice

Combine jelly and boiling water in a small bowl; mix until jelly is melted. Fill glass with ice cubes. Add jelly mixture and tonic water. Stir gently. Garnish with strawberry and lemon slice. Makes 1 serving.

ROSY

Ice cubes
2 tablespoons lemon juice
1 tablespoon Grenadine syrup
Cold sparkling water
Lemon slice

Fill glass with ice cubes. Add lemon juice and Grenadine syrup. Fill glass with sparkling water and stir gently. Garnish with lemon slice. Makes 1 serving.

ORANGE FLURRY

Ice cubes
¼ cup orange juice
½ cup cold tonic water
Orange slice

Fill glass with ice cubes. Add orange juice and tonic water. Stir gently. Garnish with orange slice. Makes 1 serving.

MINT TONIC

3 mint sprigs
½ teaspoon sugar
Crushed ice
½ teaspoon lemon juice
2 tablespoons unsweetened grapefruit juice
½ cup cold tonic water

Crush 2 mint sprigs with sugar in glass. Fill glass with crushed ice. Add lemon juice, grapefruit juice and tonic water. Stir. Garnish with remaining mint sprig. Makes 1 serving.

HOMEMADE GINGER ALE

1 qt. cold sparkling water (4 cups)

¼ cup Ginger Syrup, page 15

Ice

Pour sparkling water into a medium pitcher. Stir in Ginger Syrup. Serve over ice. Makes 1 quart.

GINGER RICKEY

Crushed ice

2 tablespoons Ginger Syrup, page 15

2 tablespoons Grenadine syrup

1 teaspoon lime juice

⅔ cup cold sparkling water

Lemon slice

Maraschino cherry

Fill glass ¼ full with crushed ice. Add Ginger Syrup, Grenadine syrup and lime juice. Fill glass with sparkling water. Stir well. Garnish with lemon slice and maraschino cherry. Makes 1 serving.

GINGERBERRY

2 tablespoons Grenadine syrup

2 tablespoons half and half

6 fresh strawberries, hulled

Ice cubes

Ginger ale

Ground ginger

Combine Grenadine syrup, half and half and strawberries in a blender. Process about 10 seconds or until smooth. Fill glass with ice cubes. Add strawberry mixture, then fill with ginger ale. Sprinkle with ginger. Makes 1 serving.

RAIL-SPLITTER

3 tablespoons lemon juice
1 teaspoon powdered sugar
Ice cubes
3/4 cup cold Ginger Beer, page 72, or purchased ginger beer
Lemon slice

Combine lemon juice and powdered sugar in glass. Stir well. Fill glass with ice cubes. Add Ginger Beer. Stir gently and garnish with lemon slice. Makes 1 serving.

MOSCOW DONKEY

Ice cubes
2 teaspoons lime juice
3/4 cup cold Ginger Beer, page 72, or purchased ginger beer
Lime slice

Fill glass with ice cubes. Add lime juice and Ginger Beer. Stir gently and garnish with lime slice. Makes 1 serving.

HOMEMADE ROOT BEER

1 (1/4-oz.) package active dry yeast (1 tablespoon)
1 cup warm water
1/4 cup root-beer concentrate
8 cups sugar
10 qts. water, room temperature

Dissolve yeast in warm water in a bowl and let stand 10 minutes. Combine root-beer concentrate and sugar in a very large container. Stir well. Add water and stir well; then add yeast mixture and stir well. Pour root beer into sterilized 1-quart bottles and cap securely. Store in a warm, draft-free place 3 to 4 days or until root beer is effervescent. Serve cold. Makes 10 quarts.

LEFT TO RIGHT: GINGERBERRY, MOSCOW DONKEY, HOMEMADE ROOT BEER, GINGER RICKEY, HOMEMADE GINGER ALE

MORE CARBONATED DRINKS

CHOCOLATE EGG CREAM

CHOCOLATE EGG CREAM

3 tablespoons Chocolate Syrup, page 15, or purchased chocolate syrup
3 tablespoons very cold milk
Cold sparkling water

Put Chocolate Syrup and milk into 8-ounce glass and stir. Fill glass with sparkling water to form a foamy head on drink. Makes 1 serving.

DOCTOR PURPLE

Ice cubes
½ cup prune juice
2 tablespoons Grenadine syrup
Cold sparkling water
Lemon wedge

Fill glass with ice cubes. Add prune juice and Grenadine syrup; stir well. Fill glass with sparkling water. Stir gently and garnish with lemon wedge. Makes 1 serving.

COCO-LEMON FIZZ

¼ cup cream of coconut
½ cup lemon sherbet, softened
4 ice cubes
1 cup bitter-lemon soda

Combine cream of coconut and sherbet in glass; mix well. Add ice cubes and fill glass with bitter-lemon soda. Makes 1 serving.

COFFEE-COLA FLIP

Crushed ice
½ cup cold strong coffee
Cola soda
2 tablespoons whipping cream

Fill glass half-full with crushed ice. Add coffee. Fill glass with cola. Float cream on top. Makes 1 serving.

ORANGE JULIA

Crushed ice
½ cup orange juice
1 teaspoon pure vanilla extract
Cold sparkling water

Fill glass half-full with crushed ice. Add orange juice and vanilla; stir. Fill glass with sparkling water. Makes 1 serving.

BLACK & TAN

Ice cubes
¾ cup cola soda
½ cup milk

Fill glass with ice cubes. Add cola, then milk. Stir. Makes 1 serving.

STRAWBERRY ICE-CREAM SODA

3 tablespoons frozen strawberries, thawed, undrained

2 scoops strawberry ice cream

3/4 cup cream soda

Whipped cream

Fresh strawberry, hulled

Mash 3 tablespoons strawberries in bottom of 14-ounce glass. Add 3 tablespoons ice cream and 2 tablespoons cream soda and stir well. Add remaining ice cream. Pour in remaining cream soda to fill glass. Top with whipped cream; garnish with strawberry. Makes 1 serving.

COLA FIZZ

2 scoops vanilla ice cream

2 tablespoons lime juice

Cola soda

Lime slice

Combine ice cream and lime juice in a blender. Process 5 seconds. Pour into glass; fill glass with cola. Garnish with lime slice and serve with a straw. Makes 1 serving.

LEMON SHERBET SODA

1/2 cup lemon sherbet, softened

1 cup cold strong tea

Cold sparkling water

Mint sprigs

Put sherbet into glass. Add tea. Fill glass with sparkling water; stir well. Garnish with mint sprigs. Makes 1 serving.

BLACK COW

1 1/4 cups root beer

1 scoop vanilla ice cream

Pour 6 tablespoons root beer into 14-ounce glass. Add 2 teaspoons ice cream and stir until creamy. Add remaining ice cream. Fill glass with remaining root beer. Makes 1 serving.

MAPLE-YOGURT ICE-CREAM SODA

2 tablespoons maple syrup

1/4 cup plain yogurt

1 scoop vanilla ice cream

Cold sparkling water

Combine maple syrup and yogurt in glass; stir well. Add ice cream and fill glass with sparkling water; stir. Makes 1 serving.

STRAWBERRY ICE-CREAM SODA

BLACK VELVET

SHANDYGAFF

¾ cup light or nonalcoholic beer

¾ cup Ginger Beer, page 72, or purchased ginger beer

Pour beer and Ginger Beer into glass. Stir gently. Makes 1 serving.

SANGAREE

1 teaspoon powdered sugar

1 tablespoon water

Ice cubes

¾ cup light or nonalcoholic beer

Freshly grated nutmeg

Dissolve powdered sugar in water in glass. Fill glass with ice cubes; add beer. Sprinkle with nutmeg. Makes 1 serving.

SHANDY PITCHER

2 cups light or nonalcoholic beer

2 cups ginger ale

2 tablespoons black currant syrup, if desired

1 lemon, sliced

Combine beer, ginger ale and black currant syrup, if desired, in a 2-quart pitcher. Add lemon slices and stir gently. Makes 1 quart.

HOT PINK BEER

1 cup light or nonalcoholic beer

½ teaspoon hot-pepper sauce

Fill glass with beer. Add hot-pepper sauce and stir. Makes 1 serving.

TOMBOY

½ cup tomato juice

⅛ teaspoon celery salt

1 teaspoon barbecue sauce

1 teaspoon lemon juice

Ice cubes

¾ cup light or nonalcoholic beer

Combine tomato juice, celery salt, barbecue sauce and lemon juice in a cocktail shaker with ice cubes. Stir well and strain into glass. Fill glass with beer. Makes 1 serving.

BLACK VELVET

¾ cup stout

¾ cup cold sparkling wine

Pour stout into champagne flute. Slowly add sparkling wine. Makes 1 serving.

中國名
unusually successful
business.

Tea

Legend has it that the Chinese emperor Shen Nung discovered tea nearly 5000 years ago, when a leaf from a tea bush fell into his bowl of boiled drinking water. The pleasures of tea were known only in Eastern lands until the early 1600s, when European traders began bringing it back from Far Eastern ports. At first, tea was rare and fabulously expensive, and was drunk only by the wealthy. But by the 1800s, it had become the inexpensive, refreshing and popular drink it is today. In fact, tea is second only to water as the world's most popular beverage. Approximately 200 million pounds of tea are imported to the United States each year—enough to make about 40 billion cups!

The tea plant is an evergreen that belongs to the camellia family; it's cultivated on plantations in tropical and subtropical climates. At one time, nearly all the tea used in the world came from China. But today, most of the tea we drink is produced in India, Sri Lanka, Indonesia, Kenya, Malawi and Tanzania.

Of the over 3000 varieties of tea, most take their names from the area where they are grown. Darjeeling, for example, comes from a region of the Himalayas of India; Assam is grown in northeastern India. Many brands of tea are actually blends—the average teabag may contain 20 to 30 different teas, all carefully selected by a master tea blender. The variations in flavor among types of tea don't come from differences in the actual tea plant, which is much the same in all parts of the world. Flavor differences result from different growing conditions—variations in soil acidity and altitude, for example—and from the processing method used after harvesting.

When tea is harvested, the top two leaves and a bud are pinched from the tips of the branches. The fresh green leaves are spread on racks in a withering loft for 12 to 24 hours, while currents of warm, dry air remove much of their moisture. Then they're rolled through special machines and sent to cool, humid oxidizing rooms, where they remain for 20 minutes to an hour (the oxidizing step is omitted for green tea and shortened for oolong tea). After that, the leaves are dried, graded, and packed for shipment.

Virtually all the tea drunk in America is *black tea.* Black tea is made from leaves that have been fully oxidized (hence the dark color); it makes a hearty, rich-colored brew. *Green tea* is not oxidized, so the leaves stay green. This type of tea is delicate-flavored and light in color. *Oolong tea,* most popular in China, is only partially oxidized. It has a greenish-brown color and makes a fairly light brew. (The familiar terms *pekoe* and *orange pekoe,* often seen on boxes of teabags, simply refer to the size of the original leaf; they don't give any indication of the flavor, quality, or origin of a tea.)

THE PERFECT CUP OF TEA

Making the perfect cup of tea is a simple matter of following these basic steps:

- Bring freshly drawn cold water to a rapid boil.
- If using a teapot, preheat it by rinsing with hot water.
- Use 1 teaspoon of tea or one teabag per cup. Loose tea can be placed directly in the teapot if the tea is strained as it is poured into the cup; otherwise, use a tea infuser.
- Pour the boiling water over the tea.
- Brew the tea for 3 to 5 minutes by the clock—don't judge by the color, since some teas are lighter than others.

Storage. Store tea in an airtight container in a cool, dry place. Do not refrigerate it.

Tea infusers. Sometimes called tea eggs or tea balls, infusers hold the loose tea in one place while allowing the water to circulate around the leaves. Some infusers are designed as sleeves or inserts to fit inside teapots; others are made for individual cups of tea and hold only a spoonful or so of tea leaves.

Serving tea. Tea can be enjoyed by itself or with additions. A teaspoonful of sugar, honey or jam adds extra flavor, as does the juice of a lemon wedge. Although many people add milk or cream to their tea, this neutralizes some of the flavor. In any case, you should never combine milk and lemon.

TYPES OF TEAS

1. *Assam* is a high-quality Indian black tea that makes a full-bodied, robust brew.
2. *Ceylon* black teas are delicate and fragrant.
3. *Darjeeling* is the finest and most delicately flavored of the Indian black teas.
4. *Lapsang souchong* has an interesting smoky flavor. This pungent, strong black tea comes from Taiwan.
5. *Oolong* tea is partially oxidized; it has a greenish-brown color with a subtle flavor and bouquet.
6. *Gunpowder* green tea comes from India, Sri Lanka (Ceylon) or Taiwan. Each leaf is rolled into a small pellet. The leaves make a pale, delicate tea.
7. *Japanese green* tea makes a light, gentle brew.
8. *Earl Grey* makes an aromatic, hearty brew. The black leaves are often scented with oil of bergamot, a citrus fruit that gives the tea a delicious flavor.
9. *Jasmine* tea is tantalizingly scented with white jasmine blossoms.

SPICY ORANGE TEA

INDIAN GINGER-SPICED TEA

1 teaspoon black tea leaves
5 thin slices fresh gingerroot
1¼ cups boiling water
Honey to taste

Combine tea and 3 slices gingerroot in a warmed teapot. Add water, cover and infuse 4 minutes. Strain into cup and add remaining 2 slices gingerroot. Sweeten with honey. Makes 1 serving.

MASALA CHAI (SPICED INDIAN TEA)

1 cup milk
2 cups water
1 teaspoon black tea leaves
3 cardamom pods
6 whole cloves
1 (2- to 3-inch) cinnamon stick

Combine milk and water in a saucepan. Bring to a boil; then remove from heat and add tea, cardamom, cloves and cinnamon stick. Cover and infuse 5 minutes. Strain into cups. Makes 3 servings.

MIDDLE-EASTERN ANISE TEA

1 teaspoon anise seeds
2 cups boiling water
2 cups hot tea

Place anise seeds in a large bowl. Add water, cover and let stand 10 minutes. Stir in tea and immediately strain into cups. Makes 4 servings.

RUSSIAN TEA

2 tablespoons black tea leaves
About 2 cups boiling water
Sugar or jam to taste
Lemon slices

Combine tea and ½ cup boiling water in a warmed small teapot. Cover and infuse 10 minutes. Pour tea essence into 2 cups and dilute with enough additional boiling water to fill cups. Sweeten with sugar or jam; serve tea with lemon slices. Makes 2 servings.

DUTCH TEA

3 egg yolks
¼ cup sugar
1 qt. milk (4 cups)
4 teaspoons black tea leaves

Place egg yolks and sugar in a small bowl and lightly beat together with a whisk. Set aside. Place milk in a saucepan. Bring to a boil; add tea, reduce heat to low and simmer 5 minutes. Strain tea-milk mixture into a large bowl. Using whisk, slowly beat in egg-yolk mixture. Makes 4 servings.

MOROCCAN MINT TEA

4 teaspoons green tea leaves
½ cup sugar
1¼ cups firmly packed spearmint sprigs
4 cups boiling water

Combine tea, sugar and spearmint sprigs in a warmed teapot; add water. Cover and infuse 5 minutes, pushing spearmint down below water level. Makes 4 servings.

CARDAMOM TEA

3 tablespoons black tea leaves
1 lemon wedge
12 cardamom pods
6 cups cold water
Milk
Sugar

Place tea and lemon wedge in a teapot. Set aside. Combine cardamom and water in a large saucepan. Bring to a boil; then reduce heat, cover and simmer 5 minutes. Remove from heat and let stand 10 minutes. Return to a boil and pour into teapot. Cover and infuse 2 to 3 minutes. Serve with milk and sugar. Makes 1½ quarts.

SPICY ORANGE TEA

8 cups water
1 (2- to 3-inch) cinnamon stick
10 whole cloves
3 tablespoons black tea leaves
¾ cup honey
3 tablespoons lemon juice
1 cup orange juice

Combine water, cinnamon stick and cloves in a large saucepan. Bring to a boil; then remove from heat and add tea. Cover and infuse 5 minutes. Combine honey, lemon juice and orange juice in another saucepan. Bring to a boil, stirring until honey is dissolved; then add to tea. Stir and strain into cups. Makes 2-½ quarts.

BASIC ICED TEA

5 teabags
4 cups cold water
Powdered sugar to taste
Mint sprigs

Combine teabags and water in a 1-quart container. Cover and refrigerate 12 hours. Sweeten each serving with powdered sugar; garnish with mint sprigs. Makes 1 quart.

SOUTHERN-STYLE ICED TEA

1 gal. water (4 qts.)
10 teabags
1 (2- to 3-inch) cinnamon stick
1 lemon, sliced
4 cups sugar

Place water in a large saucepan. Bring to a boil and add teabags, cinnamon stick and lemon slices. Reduce heat to low, cover loosely and simmer 20 minutes. Remove from heat, add sugar and stir until sugar is dissolved. Remove teabags, cinnamon stick and lemon slices. Pour tea into a large jug and refrigerate until well chilled. Makes 4 quarts.

MINTED ICED TEA

6 cups water
3 tablespoons black tea leaves
10 mint sprigs
1¼ cups sugar
1 cup orange juice
½ cup lemon juice

Combine water, tea, mint sprigs and sugar in a saucepan. Bring to a boil; then boil 1 minute, stirring until sugar is dissolved. Remove from heat, cover and infuse 10 minutes. Strain into a pitcher. Stir in orange juice and lemon juice. Refrigerate until well chilled. Makes 2 quarts.

LEFT TO RIGHT: BASIC ICED TEA, SPICY ICY TEA, ICED ANISE TEA, FIZZY ICED TEA, MINTED ICED TEA

ICED ANISE TEA

2 tablespoons anise seeds
1 cup boiling water
2 cups cold tea
1 cup milk
Sugar to taste
Crushed ice

Combine anise seeds and water in a small bowl and let stand 10 minutes. Place tea in a pitcher; strain anise mixture into pitcher. Add milk and sweeten with sugar; stir until sugar is dissolved. Refrigerate until well chilled. Serve over crushed ice. Makes 1 quart.

FIZZY ICED TEA

10 ice cubes
1½ cups sugar
⅓ cup lemon juice
4 cups cold tea
2 cups cold sparkling water

Place ice cubes in a large pitcher. Add sugar and lemon juice; stir until sugar is dissolved. Stir in tea. Stir in sparkling water and serve immediately. Makes 1½ quarts.

SPICY ICY TEA

2½ cups boiling water
2 tablespoons black tea leaves
6 whole allspice berries
1 (2- to 3-inch) cinnamon stick
¼ teaspoon freshly grated nutmeg
¾ cup sugar
1½ cups cranberry juice
½ cup orange juice
⅓ cup lemon juice
1½ cups cold water

Combine boiling water, tea, allspice, cinnamon stick and nutmeg in a large bowl. Cover and infuse 5 minutes. Strain into a pitcher, add sugar and stir until dissolved. Add cranberry juice, orange juice, lemon juice and cold water. Stir. Refrigerate until well chilled. Makes 1½ quarts.

Herbal Drinks

Delicious beverages can be made from leaves, flowers, seeds, fruits, barks and roots—in fact, almost any edible plant can be made into an herbal infusion. Often called tisanes, hot herbal teas are refreshing in their own right and are also a good caffeine-free substitute for coffee and tea. Cold herbal drinks are good thirst-quenching alternatives to carbonated beverages, and don't have the calories of fruit juices.

Individual herbs such as spearmint or chamomile make fine teas by themselves, but one of the real pleasures of herbal teas comes from using herb combinations. A favorite blend in Colonial times, for example, contained peppermint leaves mixed with cloves, nutmeg and dried orange or lemon peel. Lemon verbena with rose petals, chamomile and rosemary was another favorite combination. When experimenting with your own mixtures, decide on one predominant flavor; then add the other ingredients in proportion. The choice of herbs is entirely up to you, but to avoid confusing the flavors, it's best to use a maximum of three or four herbs.

The herbs you use may be grown in your garden, bought at the supermarket or purchased at a spice shop or health-food store. Dried herbs are usually quite inexpensive, especially when purchased by the ounce—and an ounce goes a long way. When stored in airtight containers in a cool, dry, dark place, most herbs will keep for about 6 months. Discard any herbs that have lost their aroma or have taken on a musty smell. Herbs will last longer if they are whole, not crushed, but they should be crumbled or broken up before brewing.

Many leafy herbs such as rosemary and spearmint are easily grown at home in a garden or windowbox. To store them, cut the sprigs a little above ground level when the plant is full and leafy, but before it has gone to seed. Tie the sprigs together at the cut ends with string, forming a loose bundle. Hang the bundle in a dry, dark place with good air circulation. When the leaves are completely dried and crisp (2 to 6 weeks, depending on the herb), pull them from the stems, transfer to airtight containers and store.

To dry flowering herbs such as chamomile, gather the flowers and spread them in a thin layer on paper towels. Then follow the drying steps outlined above for leafy herbs.

Herbs can be found growing wild almost anywhere, even in vacant lots or along the roadside. A number of guidebooks to edible wild herbs are available. If you gather wild herbs, choose only plants that are healthy; avoid any that have insect or fungus infestations or discolored leaves. Before drying the herbs, wash them well to remove dirt, pesticides and so on. Always refer to your guidebook if you have any doubts about the herb.

BREWING HERBAL TEAS

To brew an herbal tea, follow these steps:

- Bring freshly drawn cold water to a rapid boil.
- If using a teapot, preheat it by rinsing with hot water.
- Use about 1 teaspoon of the herb or herb combination per cup. The herbs can be placed directly in the teapot or in a tea infuser; if the tea is made in the cup, use a tea infuser.
- Pour the boiling water over the herbs.
- The brewing time will depend on the herbs. Generally, leafy herbs should be brewed for about 5 minutes. Other herbs will usually take longer. Since the color of the tea will vary considerably depending on the herb, use the clock and your personal taste as guides.
- The flavor of many herbal teas is brought out by a bit of honey or sugar. Milk or cream is not recommended.

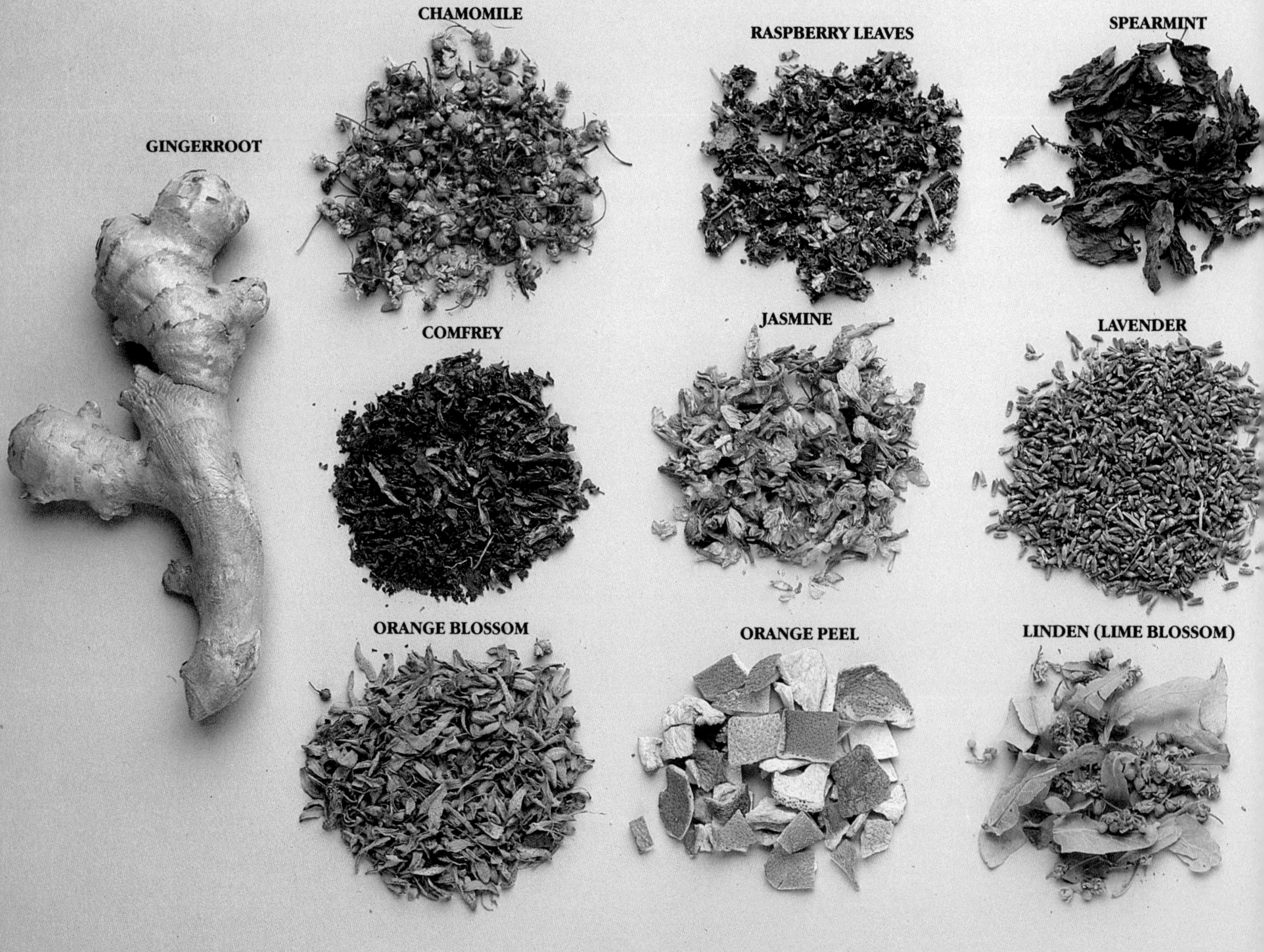

FENNEL SEEDS
ROSEHIPS
CLOVES
BURDOCK ROOT
LEMON GRASS
LEMON PEEL
SAGE
BORAGE
VERVAIN
PEPPERMINT
CHICORY
HIBISCUS

MINTED CHAMOMILE TEA

1 teaspoon dried chamomile
1 teaspoon dried leaf peppermint
2 cups boiling water
Ground cinnamon
Orange slices

Combine chamomile and peppermint in a warmed teapot. Add water, cover and infuse 5 minutes. Serve immediately. Garnish with cinnamon and orange slices. Makes 2 servings.

MIDNIGHT CHAMOMILE

SPICED MINT TEA

1/4 cup water

2 tablespoons honey

2 tablespoons chopped fresh mint

4 whole allspice berries

1/4 cup lemon juice

1/2 cup orange juice

2 cups boiling water

Combine 1/4 cup water and honey in a small saucepan. Bring to a boil, stirring until honey is dissolved; then reduce heat and simmer 5 minutes. Remove from heat; add mint and allspice. Cover and infuse 10 minutes. Strain into a bowl and add lemon juice, orange juice and boiling water. Stir well. Makes 3 servings.

ROSEHIP TISANE

1 cup halved rosehips

6 cups water

3 tablespoons sugar

Remove and discard any filaments from rosehips. Place water in a saucepan, bring to a boil and add rosehips. Reduce heat to very low, cover tightly and simmer 20 minutes. Remove from heat and let stand 3 hours. Reheat gently just until hot. Strain, add sugar and stir until dissolved. Makes 4 servings.

MATÉ

4 tablespoons maté leaves

4 cups boiling water

Sugar to taste, if desired

Place maté in a warmed teapot. Add water, cover and infuse 10 to 12 minutes. Strain; sweeten with sugar, if desired. This drink contains caffeine. Makes 4 servings.

SPEARMINT-GINSENG TEA

1 teaspoon dried leaf spearmint

1/4 teaspoon powdered ginseng root

2 whole cloves

1 cup boiling water

1 cup orange juice

Lemon slices

Combine spearmint, ginseng, cloves and water in a saucepan. Cover and infuse 5 minutes. Add orange juice and mix well. Strain into cups and garnish with lemon slices. Makes 2 servings.

MIDNIGHT CHAMOMILE

1 cup water

1 teaspoon dried chamomile

1 (2-inch) piece orange peel

1 teaspoon honey

Combine water, chamomile, orange peel and honey in a saucepan. Bring to a boil. Remove from heat, cover and infuse 5 minutes. Strain into cup and serve immediately. Makes 1 serving.

CHAMOMILE BLEND

2 rosehips

2 cups water

1 teaspoon dried lemon verbena

¼ teaspoon dried leaf rosemary

2 teaspoons dried chamomile

Honey to taste

Remove and discard any filaments from rosehips. Place water in a small saucepan. Bring to a boil and add rosehips, lemon verbena, rosemary and chamomile. Remove from heat, cover and infuse 6 minutes. Strain into cups; sweeten with honey. Makes 2 servings.

SPICED LEMON TEA

3 cups water

1 tablespoon dried lemon peel

2 teaspoons dried lemon balm

3 whole cloves

1 (2- to 3-inch) cinnamon stick

Honey to taste

Place water in a medium saucepan, bring to a boil and add lemon peel, lemon balm, cloves and cinnamon stick. Reduce heat to very low, cover and simmer 10 minutes. Strain into cups; sweeten with honey. Makes 4 servings.

YOGI TEA

1 cup water

1 (2- to 3-inch) cinnamon stick

1 thick slice fresh gingerroot

3 whole black peppercorns

3 cardamom pods

6 whole cloves

Honey to taste

Place water in a small saucepan; bring to a boil and add cinnamon stick, gingerroot, peppercorns, cardamom and cloves. Remove from heat, cover and infuse 7 minutes. Strain into cup; sweeten with honey. Makes 1 serving.

CHAMOMILE TODDY

2¼ cups water

4 teaspoons dried chamomile

2 tablespoons lemon juice

2 tablespoons brandy

¼ cup apricot jam

Place water in a saucepan, bring to a boil and add chamomile. Remove from heat, cover and infuse 5 minutes. Stir in lemon juice and brandy. Strain into cups; stir 1 tablespoon jam into each cup. Makes 4 servings.

LEFT TO RIGHT: CHAMOMILE TODDY, ICED SPICED MINT TEA

COLONIAL BLEND

1 cup water

1 teaspoon dried leaf peppermint

2 whole cloves

⅛ teaspoon freshly grated nutmeg

½ teaspoon grated orange peel

Honey to taste

Place water in a small saucepan, bring to a boil and add peppermint, cloves, nutmeg and orange peel. Remove from heat, cover and infuse 5 minutes. Strain into cup; sweeten with honey. Makes 1 serving.

ZINGER

3 rosehips, halved

1 cup water

1 teaspoon dried hibiscus leaves

½ teaspoon dried orange peel

1 teaspoon dried lemon grass

½ teaspoon dried leaf peppermint

½ teaspoon dried leaf spearmint

1 teaspoon dried cherry bark

Honey to taste

Remove and discard any filaments from rosehips. Place water in a small saucepan; bring to a boil and add rosehips, hibiscus leaves, orange peel, lemon grass, peppermint, spearmint and cherry bark. Remove from heat, cover and infuse 6 minutes. Strain into cup; sweeten with honey. Makes 1 serving.

GINGER DRINKS

GINGER BEER

1 cup coarsely grated fresh gingerroot

3 cups boiling water

3 cups cold water

½ cup lemon juice

6 whole cloves

1½ cups sugar

Place gingerroot in a blender or a food processor fitted with a metal blade and process until pulped. Put pulp in a bowl and add boiling water. Cover and let stand 2 hours. Strain through cheesecloth into a large bowl, squeezing to extract all liquid; discard ginger. Add cold water, lemon juice and cloves to liquid in bowl. Stir well and let stand 1 hour. Strain liquid through cheesecloth into a pitcher. Add sugar and stir until dissolved. Refrigerate until well chilled. Makes 1½ quarts.

GINGERADE

1 cup coarsely grated fresh gingerroot

4 lemons, very thinly sliced

8 cups boiling water

2 cups lemon juice

Powdered sugar to taste

Crushed ice

Mint sprigs

Place gingerroot in a blender or a food processor fitted with a metal blade and process until pulped. Combine pulp and lemon slices in a large bowl. Add water, cover and let stand 5 minutes. Strain through cheesecloth into a large pitcher and refrigerate until well chilled. Stir in lemon juice; sweeten with powdered sugar. Serve over crushed ice. Garnish with mint sprigs. Makes 2½ quarts.

GINGER-MINT CUP

2 cups finely chopped fresh mint

2 cups sugar

2 cups water

⅛ teaspoon salt

8 cups Gingerade, this page, or ginger ale

Crushed ice

Mint sprigs

Combine chopped mint, sugar, water and salt in a saucepan. Bring to a boil, stirring until sugar is dissolved. Reduce heat and simmer, stirring, 3 minutes. Remove from heat; cool. Strain into a large pitcher. Add Gingerade or ginger ale and refrigerate until well chilled. Serve over crushed ice. Garnish with mint sprigs. Makes 2½ quarts.

GINGER MINTADE

1 tablespoon grated lemon peel

½ cup chopped fresh mint

½ cup lemon juice

½ cup boiling water

2 tablespoons sugar

¼ cup orange juice

8 cups Gingerade, this page, or ginger ale

Crushed ice

Mint sprigs

Combine lemon peel, chopped mint, lemon juice, water and sugar in a large pitcher. Stir until sugar is dissolved. Let stand 1 hour. Add orange juice and Gingerade or ginger ale. Stir well. Serve over crushed ice. Garnish with mint sprigs. Makes 2½ quarts.

GINGER DRINK

1 tablespoon molasses

1 tablespoon finely chopped fresh gingerroot

2 teaspoons lemon juice

2 cups water

Combine molasses, gingerroot, lemon juice and water in a small saucepan. Bring to a boil. Remove from heat, cover and let stand 5 minutes. Strain into mugs; serve immediately. Makes 2 servings.

KOREAN GINGER TEA

⅓ cup very thinly sliced fresh gingerroot

5 cups water

¾ cup sugar

½ teaspoon ground cinnamon

1 tablespoon pine nuts (pignoli)

1½ tablespoons chopped walnuts

2 dates, pitted and coarsely chopped

Combine gingerroot and water in a saucepan. Bring to a boil; then reduce heat, cover and simmer 20 minutes. Add sugar and cinnamon; stir until sugar is dissolved. Strain into cups; add some pine nuts, walnuts and dates to each serving. Makes 6 servings.

GINGER-LEMON DRINK

2 tablespoons finely chopped fresh gingerroot

1 teaspoon whole black peppercorns

10 cups water

2½ cups sugar

1½ cups lemon juice

Combine gingerroot, peppercorns and 8 cups water in a saucepan. Bring to a boil; then reduce heat and simmer 4 minutes. Remove from heat and cool. Strain through cheesecloth into a large pitcher. Set aside. Combine sugar and remaining 2 cups water in a small saucepan. Heat over low heat, stirring, just until sugar is dissolved. Pour into pitcher. Add lemon juice and stir well. Makes 3 quarts.

LEFT TO RIGHT: GINGER-LEMON DRINK, GINGERADE, GINGER DRINK, GINGER-MINT CUP, GINGER MINTADE

Coffee

Arab traders in Ethiopia brought coffee to the Middle East in the 15th century. By the 17th century, coffee had become a popular drink in Europe; coffeehouses sprang up and quickly became lively centers of discussion and debate. The tradition soon spread to the colonies—Boston's Green Dragon coffeehouse is said to be the place where the Boston Tea Party of 1773 was planned. So popular is coffee in modern America that we drink over 440 million cups of it daily.

Most coffee beans today are the fruit of the evergreen tree *Coffea arabica*. To produce the best beans, the tree must be planted in rich, well-drained soil and receive only a few hours of direct sunlight every day. The temperature must remain between 55°F (15°C) and about 80°F (25°); if it falls outside this range, the beans will be damaged. Finally, the trees need just the right amount of rain—about 70 inches a year.

Fortunately for coffee-lovers, mountainous regions with a tropical or subtropical climate meet the coffee tree's requirements perfectly. Colombia and Brazil in South America, Jamaica in the Caribbean, some Central American countries, and Kenya, Tanzania and Uganda in Africa all grow and export coffee. Some coffee is also grown in Hawaii.

In the wild, coffee trees may reach about 20 feet in height, but on the plantations they're pruned to a height of just 5 feet. The trees bear small white flowers that fall off after only a few days, leaving clusters of "cherries", or coffee beans. The cherries ripen slowly, turning a rusty red. After picking, the ripe cherries must be husked. This is sometimes done by sun-drying the cherries, then removing the pulpy husks; another method involves soaking the cherries in water to soften the husks, then removing them.

After drying, the green coffee beans are roasted and packaged. If the beans are to be decaffeinated, however, they're subjected to either the solvent or water method of decaffeination before roasting. In the solvent method, the beans are placed in a rotating drum and exposed to a mixture of steam and a solvent to force out the caffeine. The beans are then dried and roasted. In the water method, the beans are soaked in hot water to remove the oils and caffeine. The soaking liquid is separated from the beans, and a solvent is added to it to extract the caffeine. Finally, the caffeine-free liquid is returned to the beans, which reabsorb the oils.

A word of caution: The caffeine in coffee does not in any way counteract the adverse effects of alcohol on reaction time and driving skill.

THE PERFECT CUP OF COFFEE

To make the perfect cup of coffee, start with the best, freshest ingredients and follow the directions for your particular coffee-maker.

The roast. Roasting brings out the flavor and aroma of coffee beans. As the beans are roasted, they turn darker and their surface becomes oily. The higher the temperature or the longer the roasting period, the darker and oilier the beans become—and the stronger their flavor. *French* or *Continental* roast beans have a dark-brown color and an oily surface; their taste is strong and rich. *American* roast beans, often called "regular" roast, are dry-surfaced and medium-brown in color. *Cinnamon* roast beans also have a dry surface, but they're paler than American roast beans—a light cinnamon-brown. They make a mild coffee.

The blend. As is the case with teas and herbs, many different coffees and coffee roasts have complementary flavors. Most preground packaged coffees are blends. Gourmet stores often offer a "house blend" and will usualy be happy to help you experiment with your own blends.

The grind. Coffee beans must be ground before brewing to release their flavor when boiling water is added. Coffee is best when made with freshly ground beans; inexpensive electric grinders are easily available. Every coffeepot or machine works best with a particular grind. As a rule, the longer the coffee will be in contact with the water, the coarser the grind should be.

Storage. Roasted whole coffee beans can be stored in a tightly covered container about 3 months at room temperature, longer in the freezer. Ground coffee should be kept tightly covered and used within a week.

Making the coffee. No matter what kind of coffee-maker you use, the proportion of ground coffee to water should always be 2 level tablespoons (1 official coffee measure) to 6 ounces (3/4 cup) water. For weaker coffee, dilute the coffee with hot water after you make it. Always use the correct grind; always start with a spotlessly clean coffee-maker and fresh cold water. Serve the coffee immediately. If you must reheat coffee, do so over gentle heat—and never let it boil.

CAFFÈ CON CIOCCOLATO (Italian Coffee with Chocolate)

2 cups hot strong coffee

2 cups hot Traditional Cocoa, page 87

Whipped cream

Grated orange peel

Combine ½ cup coffee and ½ cup cocoa in each of 4 mugs. Top with whipped cream; sprinkle with orange peel. Makes 4 servings.

CAFÉ ROYALE

¾ cup hot strong coffee

4 teaspoons brandy

1 sugar cube

Pour coffee into warmed mug. Float 2 teaspoons brandy on coffee. Put remaining 2 teaspoons brandy into a tablespoon with sugar cube. Warm spoon over hot coffee. With a match, carefully ignite brandy in teaspoon. Slowly lower spoon into coffee to ignite floating brandy. Wait 1 minute after flame has died before drinking. Makes 1 serving.

CAFÉ TOULOUSE

½ pint whipping cream (1 cup)

2 tablespoons powdered sugar

1 teaspoon pure vanilla extract

2 egg whites

4¼ cups hot strong coffee

Place cream in a bowl and beat until very thick. Add powdered sugar and vanilla; continue to beat until stiff. In a large bowl, using clean, dry beaters, beat egg whites until they form soft peaks. Fold whipped cream into egg whites. Divide mixture among 6 mugs; fill with coffee. Makes 6 servings.

CAFÉ BRÛLOT

Rinds of 2 oranges

Rinds of 2 lemons

1 (2- to 3-inch) cinnamon stick

12 whole cloves

6 tablespoons sugar

1 cup brandy

1 cup Triple Sec or Cointreau

2 cups hot strong coffee

Remove as much white pith from orange and lemon rinds as possible. Discard pith; cut remainder of rinds into thin slivers. Combine slivered rinds, cinnamon stick, cloves, sugar, brandy and Triple Sec or Cointreau in a chafing dish over canned heat. Stir until sugar is dissolved. With a match, carefully ignite spirits. Gradually stir in coffee as spirits burn. Continue stirring gently until flames die. Makes 4 servings.

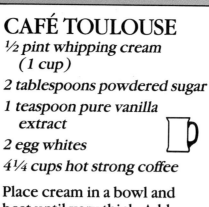

VIENNESE COFFEE

4 oz. (4 squares) semisweet chocolate

1 tablespoon sugar

¼ cup whipping cream

4 cups hot strong coffee

Whipped cream

Grated orange peel

Melt chocolate in a heavy saucepan over low heat. Stir in sugar and whipping cream. Beat in coffee with a whisk, ½ cup at a time; continue to beat until frothy. Top with whipped cream and sprinkle with orange peel. Makes 1½ quarts.

MEXICAN COFFEE

1 cup water

3 tablespoons coarsely ground coffee

1 small (about 1½-inch) cinnamon stick

Dark brown sugar to taste

Place water in a heavy saucepan and bring to a boil. Add coffee and stir well. Add cinnamon stick. Return to a boil; then remove from heat until bubbling stops. Return to heat; return to a boil. Remove from heat, strain into mug and sweeten with brown sugar. Makes 1 serving.

CAJUN COFFEE

3 cups hot strong coffee

6 tablespoons molasses

6 tablespoons dark rum, if desired

Whipped cream

Freshly grated nutmeg

Combine coffee and molasses in a saucepan. Heat, stirring, until molasses is dissolved and coffee is very hot. Do not allow to boil. If desired, place 1 tablespoon rum in each mug. Add coffee. Top with whipped cream; sprinkle with nutmeg. Do not stir before drinking. Makes 6 servings.

LEFT TO RIGHT: VIENNESE COFFEE, CAFÉ TOULOUSE, CAFFÈ CON CIOCCOLATO, CAFÉ BRÛLOT, CAJUN COFFEE

ESPRESSO ROMANO

¼ cup finely ground coffee

1½ cups cold water

2 strips lemon peel

Fill filter section of a steam-pressure coffeepot with coffee. Fill base of coffeepot with water. Place filter in base and screw on top portion of coffeepot. Heat over medium heat until coffee begins to bubble into top portion. Reduce heat to low and simmer until bubbling stops. Serve immediately. Garnish with lemon peel. Makes 2 servings.

TURKISH COFFEE

¾ cup water

1 tablespoon sugar

1 tablespoon pulverized coffee

1 cardamom pod

Combine water and sugar in an *ibrik* or small saucepan. Bring to a boil; then remove from heat and add coffee and cardamom. Stir well and return to heat. When coffee foams up, remove from heat and let grounds settle. Repeat twice more. Pour into cups; let grounds settle before drinking. Makes 2 servings.

SESAME DEMITASSE

2 cups hot coffee

1½ tablespoons honey

1½ tablespoons sugar

1½ tablespoons sesame seeds

Combine coffee, honey, sugar and sesame seeds in a saucepan. Stir until honey and sugar are dissolved; then cover and simmer 2 minutes. Strain into cups. Makes 4 servings.

LEFT TO RIGHT: TURKISH COFFEE WITH *IBRIK*, ESPRESSO ROMANO, CAPPUCCINO

EINSPÄNNER (German Coffee with Whipped Cream)

5 cups hot strong coffee
Sugar to taste
Whipped cream

Pour coffee into stemmed glasses and sweeten with sugar. Stir until sugar is dissolved. Top with whipped cream. Makes 6 servings.

CAFÉ AU LAIT

1 ½ cups milk
1 ½ cups hot strong coffee
Sugar to taste

Place milk in a saucepan and heat until bubbles form. Pour into a small pitcher. Pour milk and coffee simultaneously into cups; sweeten with sugar. Makes 4 servings.

CAPPUCCINO I

3 cups milk
3 cups hot Espresso Romano, this page
Sugar to taste
Ground cinnamon

Put milk in a pitcher and steam with steam pipe of an espresso machine. Pour espresso into cups. Add milk; sweeten with sugar. Stir and sprinkle with cinnamon. Makes 6 servings.

CAPPUCCINO II

1 ¾ cups cold milk
1 ¾ cups hot strong coffee
Cocoa powder

Pour milk into cups, then add coffee. Do not stir. Sprinkle with cocoa. Makes 4 servings.

RUSSIAN ICED COFFEE

5½ cups cold strong coffee
¼ cup half and half
2 tablespoons sugar
2 tablespoons any flavor liqueur
6 scoops vanilla ice cream
Grated chocolate

Combine coffee, half and half and sugar in a pitcher. Stir until sugar is dissolved. Refrigerate until well chilled. Stir in liqueur. Pour into 6 glasses; add 1 scoop ice cream to each glass. Sprinkle with grated chocolate. Makes 6 servings.

MAZAGRAN (Spanish Iced Coffee)

1 cup cold strong coffee
⅔ cup cold water
3 tablespoons brandy
¼ cup sugar
1 teaspoon lemon juice
Ice cubes

Combine coffee, water, brandy, sugar and lemon juice in a pitcher. Stir until sugar is dissolved. Serve over ice cubes. Makes 2 servings.

ICY SPICED COFFEE

2½ cups hot strong coffee
2 (2- to 3-inch) cinnamon sticks
4 whole cloves
4 whole allspice berries
⅔ cup whipping cream
6 ice cubes
Sugar to taste
Ice cubes

Combine coffee, cinnamon sticks, cloves and allspice in a bowl. Cool to room temperature; then refrigerate until well chilled. Strain into a blender. Add cream and 6 ice cubes; sweeten with sugar. Process on low speed about 40 seconds or until creamy and frothy. Serve immediately over ice cubes. Makes 4 servings.

COFFEE COOLER

6 tablespoons honey
2 tablespoons sugar
4 cups cold strong coffee
½ cup half and half
¼ teaspoon ground ginger
2 egg whites
Cracked ice

Dissolve honey and sugar in coffee in a bowl. Refrigerate until well chilled. Combine coffee mixture, half and half, ginger and egg whites in a blender. Process on low speed 30 seconds. Serve over cracked ice. Makes 4 servings.

ICED COFFEE WITH CREAM

1 cup cold strong coffee
1 cup half and half
1 cup milk
Sugar to taste
Ice cubes

Combine coffee, half and half and milk in a pitcher. Sweeten with sugar and stir well. Serve over ice cubes. Makes 4 servings.

PEANUT-BUTTER CAFÉ

1 cup cold strong coffee
¼ cup milk
1½ teaspoons peanut butter
3 tablespoons sugar
1 cup cracked ice
Ice cubes

Combine coffee, milk, peanut butter, sugar and cracked ice in a blender. Process on high speed about 2 minutes or until foamy. Serve over ice cubes. Makes 2 servings.

BERLIN ICED COFFEE

1 cup cold strong coffee
1 scoop chocolate ice cream
Whipped cream
Cocoa powder

Pour coffee into glass. Add ice cream. Top with whipped cream and sprinkle with cocoa. Makes 1 serving.

LEFT TO RIGHT: ICY SPICED COFFEE, BERLIN ICED COFFEE

DIJON

Chocolate

One of the world's favorite flavorings, chocolate has been popular ever since the Aztec Indians introduced it to early explorers. Among the Aztecs, the cacao bean—from which chocolate is made—was so highly valued that it was used as currency. Chocolate is no longer legal tender in the modern world, but it's still a valued commodity: Americans consume more than 9 pounds of chocolate per person every year.

Most of today's chocolate starts with beans from cacao-tree plantations in tropical West Africa and Brazil. The trees bear large pods, each containing from 20 to 40 beans. After being removed from the pods, the beans are dried and shipped to processing plants all over the world.

In processing, the beans are ground to form a thick liquid that's about 50 percent oil. To make powdered cocoa, the liquid is pressed to remove the oil (called "cocoa butter"), leaving unsweetened powder behind. To make bar chocolate, whether for baking or eating, the liquid is enriched with additional cocoa butter; if the chocolate is to be sweet, sugar is also added. Next, the mixture is poured into a container where a very heavy roller moves back and forth, constantly mixing and smoothing. The chocolate is then poured out, shaped into bars and cooled.

Hot cocoa is made from a mixture of unsweetened cocoa powder, sugar and milk or water. Hot chocolate is made from melted bar chocolate, sugar if the chocolate is unsweetened and milk or water. Hot chocolate is thicker and creamier than cocoa—but both are soothing, delicious drinks.

Whether you're making cocoa or chocolate, be sure that the milk or water is very hot but not boiling when it is added to the chocolate. Beat it in with a whisk and continue to whisk until well blended. This will make the drink light and frothy and keep a skin from forming as the liquid heats. Whipped cream is the classic garnish for hot chocolate drinks, although many prefer a marshmallow or two.

Cocoa powder does not dissolve well in cold liquids, so cold chocolate drinks are generally made with melted and cooled bar chocolate or with chocolate syrup. Commercial chocolate powders made to be stirred into cold milk are available, but these are often as much as 75 percent sugar. They are not good substitutes for chocolate in the recipes given here.

One of the most intriguing things about chocolate is its affinity for other flavors. Use the Traditional Cocoa recipe on page 87 as a starting point for experimentation. For example, you might try adding a teaspoon of freshly grated orange peel or three whole cloves when you add the milk. A teaspoon or two of a liqueur or fruit-flavored brandy will add a sophisticated touch to any chocolate drink.

TRADITIONAL COCOA

BLOWTORCH

¾ cup hot Traditional Cocoa, this page
1 tablespoon peppermint schnapps
1 tablespoon whipped cream

Pour hot cocoa into mug. Add schnapps and stir. Top with whipped cream. Makes 1 serving.

COCOA ROYALE

1 teaspoon dried leaf mint
1 qt. milk (4 cups)
5 tablespoons unsweetened cocoa powder
⅓ cup sugar
⅛ teaspoon salt
¼ cup water

Combine mint and milk in a medium saucepan. Heat, stirring, until hot. Remove from heat, cover and set aside. Combine cocoa, sugar, salt and water in another medium saucepan. Bring to a boil over medium heat, then reduce heat and simmer, stirring, 2 minutes. Strain mint-milk mixture into cocoa mixture. Cook, stirring, until liquid is just at the boiling point. Makes 4 servings.

TRADITIONAL COCOA

5 tablespoons unsweetened cocoa powder

⅓ cup sugar

⅛ teaspoon salt

¼ cup water

1 pint milk (2 cups)

1 pint half and half (2 cups)

1 teaspoon pure vanilla extract

Whipped cream

Combine cocoa, sugar, salt and water in a medium saucepan. Bring to a boil over medium heat; then reduce heat and simmer, stirring, 2 minutes. Stir in milk, half and half and vanilla. Heat, stirring, until cocoa is just at the boiling point. Garnish with whipped cream. Makes 4 servings.

CHOCOLATE-CHERRY STEAMER

1 qt. milk (4 cups)

6 tablespoons Chocolate Syrup, page 15, or purchased chocolate syrup

⅛ teaspoon salt

½ teaspoon almond extract

½ teaspoon cherry extract

Whipped cream

Maraschino cherries

Shaved chocolate

Combine milk, Chocolate Syrup and salt in a 2-quart saucepan. Heat until milk just begins to steam. Stir in almond extract and cherry extract. Garnish with whipped cream, maraschino cherries and shaved chocolate. Makes 4 servings.

YOGURT HOT COCOA

6 tablespoons unsweetened cocoa powder

6 tablespoons sugar

⅛ teaspoon salt

½ cup water

2½ cups milk

2½ cups plain yogurt

1 teaspoon pure vanilla extract

Marshmallows

Combine cocoa, sugar, salt and water in a medium saucepan. Bring to a boil over medium heat; then reduce heat and simmer, stirring, 2 minutes. Stir in milk and simmer, stirring, 2 minutes. Whisk in yogurt and simmer, stirring, 2 minutes. Remove from heat and stir in vanilla. Beat with a whisk until frothy. Garnish with marshmallows. Makes 6 servings.

MINTED HOT COCOA

¾ cup hot Traditional Cocoa, this page

4 teaspoons Triple Sec or Cointreau

1 sugar cube

Pour hot cocoa into mug. Float 2 teaspoons Triple Sec or Cointreau on cocoa. Put remaining 2 teaspoons Triple Sec or Cointreau into a tablespoon with sugar cube. Warm spoon over hot cocoa. With a match, carefully ignite liqueur in teaspoon. Slowly lower spoon into cocoa to ignite floating liqueur. Wait 1 minute after flame has died before drinking. Makes 1 serving.

MOCHA CHOCOLATE

1 oz. (1 square) unsweetened chocolate

3 tablespoons sugar

1½ cups milk

⅛ teaspoon salt

1½ cups hot, very strong coffee

Whipped cream

Freshly grated nutmeg

Combine chocolate, sugar and ½ cup milk in top half of a double boiler over simmering water. Cook, stirring, until chocolate is melted. Add salt and remaining 1 cup milk and simmer, stirring occasionally, 10 minutes. Beat with a whisk or hand beater until frothy. Slowly beat in coffee. Garnish with whipped cream and nutmeg. Makes 2 servings.

INSTANT COCOA MIX

1 (1-lb.) pkg. instant nonfat dry milk

1 cup sugar

¾ cup unsweetened cocoa powder

¼ teaspoon salt

Sift dry milk, sugar, cocoa and salt together twice. Store in a tightly covered container in a cool place. Makes about 10 cups (enough for 30 servings).

To serve:

⅓ cup Instant Cocoa Mix

½ cup very hot water

Combine cocoa mix and water in mug; stir well. Makes 1 serving.

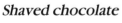

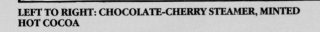

LEFT TO RIGHT: CHOCOLATE-CHERRY STEAMER, MINTED HOT COCOA

SWISS HOT COCOA

¾ cup unsweetened cocoa powder
⅔ cup sugar
1 qt. milk (4 cups)
1½ cups hot strong coffee
½ cup brandy or cherry-flavored liqueur
Whipped cream

Combine cocoa and sugar in a 2-quart saucepan. Stir in milk. Heat, stirring, until very hot but not boiling. Remove from heat and stir in coffee and brandy or liqueur. Cool slightly. Garnish with whipped cream. Makes 8 servings.

RUSSIAN HOT CHOCOLATE

12 oz. (12 squares) unsweetened chocolate

¼ cup hot water

4 cups boiling water

¼ cup sugar

6 tablespoons half and half

Whipped cream

Melt chocolate in top half of a double boiler over simmering water. Add hot water and beat well with a whisk. Add boiling water, beat well with whisk and return to a boil. Remove from heat, add sugar and beat with whisk until sugar is dissolved. Stir in half and half. Garnish with whipped cream. Makes 6 servings.

FRENCH HOT CHOCOLATE

1 cup milk

2 oz. (2 squares) semisweet chocolate

1 egg yolk

Heat milk in a small saucepan until very hot but not boiling. Pour ¾ cup of the hot milk into a mug and set aside. Add chocolate to remaining ¼ cup milk in saucepan. Heat over low heat, stirring, until chocolate is melted. Pour reserved ¾ cup milk back into saucepan. Remove from heat and stir well. Beat egg yolk in a small bowl; add 1 tablespoon chocolate milk and mix well. Pour mixture back into saucepan; beat with a whisk or hand beater until frothy. Makes 1 serving.

GERMAN HOT CHOCOLATE

2 egg yolks

1 tablespoon cold water

2 oz. (2 squares) semisweet chocolate

1 qt. milk (4 cups)

⅛ teaspoon salt

1 tablespoon sugar

1 teaspoon pure vanilla extract

Beat together egg yolks and water in a small bowl. Set aside. Melt chocolate in top half of a double boiler over simmering water; set aside. Combine milk, salt, sugar and vanilla in a 2-quart saucepan. Stir well and bring just to the boiling point over high heat. Beat in melted chocolate with a whisk or hand beater, then remove chocolate milk from heat. Beat 2 tablespoons chocolate milk into egg-yolk mixture; pour mixture back into saucepan, beating constantly. Return saucepan to heat and heat until chocolate is very hot; do not allow to boil. Makes 4 servings.

HOT CHOCOLATE ESPAÑOL

1 pint milk (2 cups)

2 oz. sweet baking chocolate, coarsely chopped

½ teaspoon ground cinnamon

2 eggs, beaten

Combine milk, chocolate and cinnamon in top half of a double boiler over simmering water. Cook, stirring, until chocolate is melted. Add eggs and beat with a whisk or hand beater until mixture is thick. Do not allow to boil. Makes 2 servings.

BRAZILIAN HOT CHOCOLATE

1 oz. sweet baking chocolate

¼ cup sugar

⅛ teaspoon salt

1 cup boiling water

½ cup hot milk

½ cup hot half and half

1½ cups hot strong coffee

1 teaspoon pure vanilla extract

¼ teaspoon ground cinnamon

Combine chocolate, sugar and salt in top half of a double boiler over simmering water. Cook, stirring, until chocolate is melted; then stir in water. Cook, stirring, 4 minutes. Add milk, half and half and coffee. Beat with a whisk or hand beater until frothy. Add vanilla and cinnamon; whisk well. Makes 3 servings.

MEXICAN HOT CHOCOLATE

1 (4-oz.) pkg. sweet baking chocolate

2 oz. (2 squares) unsweetened chocolate

1 qt. milk (4 cups)

1 (3-inch) cinnamon stick

1½ tablespoons sugar

½ teaspoon almond extract

Melt sweet baking chocolate and unsweetened chocolate in top half of a double boiler over simmering water. Combine milk and cinnamon stick in a medium saucepan and heat until very hot but not boiling. Pour into melted chocolate and stir well. Add sugar and almond extract; stir well again. Beat with a whisk or hand beater until frothy. Remove cinnamon stick. Makes 4 servings.

LEFT TO RIGHT: FRENCH HOT CHOCOLATE, BRAZILIAN HOT CHOCOLATE

COLD CHOCOLATE DRINKS

BAVARIAN CHOCOLATE

1 ice cube

3 tablespoons Chocolate Syrup, page 15, or purchased chocolate syrup

¾ cup cold strong coffee

1 scoop vanilla ice cream

Whipped cream

Put ice cube and Chocolate Syrup in glass. Add coffee and stir well. Add ice cream and top with whipped cream. Makes 1 serving.

HAPPY MARRIAGE

1½ cups cold Traditional Cocoa, page 87

½ cup cold strong coffee

2 teaspoons sugar

2 tablespoons brandy

Whipped cream

Combine cold cocoa and coffee in a bowl. Beat with a whisk or hand beater until frothy. Stir in sugar and brandy. Garnish with whipped cream. Makes 2 servings.

CHOCOLATE MALTED

1 cup milk

2 tablespoons Chocolate Syrup, page 15, or purchased chocolate syrup

2 scoops chocolate ice cream

2 teaspoons malted-milk powder

Combine milk, Chocolate Syrup, ice cream and malted-milk powder in a blender. Process until smooth and thick. Serve with a straw. Makes 1 serving.

CHOCOLATE COOLER

1 scoop chocolate ice cream

1 cup cold sparkling water

3 tablespoons Chocolate Syrup, page 15, or purchased chocolate syrup

3 tablespoons whipping cream

Combine ice cream, sparkling water, Chocolate Syrup and cream in a blender. Process about 30 seconds or until smooth. Makes 2 servings.

SPANISH CHOCOLATE MILK

3 oz. (3 squares) unsweetened chocolate

2 tablespoons unsalted butter

¾ cup sugar

½ teaspoon ground cinnamon

½ teaspoon freshly grated nutmeg

1 cup hot strong coffee

1 tablespoon pure vanilla extract

1 qt. milk (4 cups)

Melt together chocolate and butter in top half of a double boiler over simmering water. Stir in sugar, cinnamon and nutmeg. Stir in coffee, bring to a boil and boil 3 minutes. Remove from heat and cool. Stir in vanilla. Pour milk into a pitcher and add chocolate mixture. Stir well. Makes 6 servings.

CHOCOLATE-ORANGE COOLER

1 cup orange juice

1 tablespoon unsweetened cocoa powder

2 teaspoons sugar

¼ teaspoon pure vanilla extract

Crushed ice

Combine orange juice, cocoa, sugar and vanilla in a blender. Process about 20 seconds or until smooth. Pour over crushed ice in glass and serve immediately. Makes 1 serving.

RUSSIAN ICED CHOCOLATE

12 oz. (12 squares) unsweetened chocolate

¼ cup hot water

5 cups boiling water

¼ cup sugar

¼ cup half and half

2 tablespoons any flavor liqueur

Whipped cream

Grated chocolate

Melt unsweetened chocolate in top half of a double boiler over simmering water. Add hot water and beat well with a whisk. Add boiling water, stir well with whisk and return to a boil. Remove from heat, add sugar and beat with whisk until sugar is dissolved. Stir in half and half. Pour into a pitcher and refrigerate 2 hours or until well chilled. Stir in liqueur. Garnish with whipped cream and grated chocolate. Makes 6 servings.

Dairy Drinks

A snack of milk and cookies may bring back fond memories of childhood, but many of today's modern dairy drinks have a truly adult sophistication. Even better, dairy drinks are always appropriate. Nutritious breakfast drinks, refreshing thirst-quenchers, milkshake treats, elegant fruit beverages, party eggnogs, soothing bedtime drinks—no matter what the occasion, there's a good dairy drink for it.

Because milk is basically bland, it's compatible with an almost infinite number of flavors. Fruits, nuts, chocolate and spices can all be combined with milk to make delicious—and nutritious—drinks. If you're concerned about calories or cholesterol, you can substitute skim milk or low-fat milk for whole milk without affecting the drink.

When making hot milk drinks, never let the milk boil; heat it only until bubbles form around the edges and steam starts to rise. Boiled milk forms an unappetizing skin on the surface—and once it begins to boil, it boils over very quickly.

Shakes. Depending on where you live, you may call a milkshake a frappé, a frosted, a thick shake or a cabinet. In each case, what you want is a creamy, delicious mixture of milk, ice cream and fruit or a flavored syrup, all blended together into a thick, frosty mixture. No longer just for teenagers, milkshakes are now part of adult entertaining.

Yogurt drinks. The rich, tangy flavor of yogurt can be enjoyed in many drinks. Some, such as the remarkably refreshing lassi from India, rely on plain yogurt for their flavor; others add fruit and other flavorings. Like milk, yogurt combines well with almost anything.

Buttermilk drinks. Those who enjoy yogurt-based drinks will probably also enjoy drinks made with buttermilk. At one time a byproduct of butter-making, buttermilk is now made by culturing skim milk to produce a low-calorie beverage with a characteristic tangy, full-bodied flavor. Buttermilk drinks, though perhaps unusual, are also intriguingly delicious.

Soymilk. Made from soybeans, soymilk is a nutritious alternative to cow's milk. It's particularly valued by those who cannot digest milk easily. To prepare soymilk, simply follow the directions given on the packaged natural soya powder sold at health-food stores. In general, you can substitute an equivalent amount of soymilk in recipes calling for milk, but some experimentation may be needed.

Eggnogs. Traditionally served during the Christmas season, eggnogs are delicious all year round. When fruit is added, they take on a new dimension—try an eggnog for breakfast in a hurry or for a surprisingly refreshing hot-weather drink.

When making eggnogs, milkshakes or any other cold dairy drink, always start with well-chilled ingredients. And no matter what dairy drink you make, always serve it at once.

CHOCOLATE-PEPPERMINT SHAKE

CAMBRIC TEA

1 sugar cube

¼ cup whipping cream

1 tablespoon hot tea

½ cup boiling water

Put sugar cube in cup. Add cream; let stand 1 minute. Add tea and water and stir gently. Makes 1 serving.

NIGHTCAP

1 teaspoon honey

1 cup milk

¼ teaspoon pure vanilla extract

Put honey in mug and set aside in a warm place. Combine milk and vanilla in a small saucepan and heat, stirring, until milk just begins to steam; do not allow to boil. Pour into mug and stir well. Makes 1 serving.

ALMOND MILK

½ cup unsalted roasted almonds

¼ teaspoon almond extract

1 qt. milk (4 cups)

1 vanilla bean

1 cup sugar

Ice cubes

Drop almonds into a saucepan filled with boiling water and blanch 30 seconds. Drain almonds well, then rub in a towel to remove skins. Process almonds and almond extract in a blender until nuts are very finely ground. Combine milk and almond mixture in a saucepan. Bring just to the boiling point over medium heat, stirring. Remove from heat; add vanilla bean and sugar. Stir until sugar is dissolved. Reheat, then strain through cheesecloth into a pitcher and refrigerate until well chilled. Serve over ice cubes. Makes 1 quart.

LEFT TO RIGHT: INDIAN SPICED MILK, ALMOND MILK, CAMBRIC TEA, ORANGE ALMOND MILK, NIGHTCAP, SAFFRON MILK

INDIAN SPICED MILK

15 whole black peppercorns

3 tablespoons sugar

Seeds from 3 cardamom pods

½ cup golden seedless raisins

⅓ cup unsalted almonds

1 cup water

1 pint milk (2 cups)

Process peppercorns in a blender until pureed. Add sugar, cardamom, raisins, almonds and water. Process until finely pureed. Add milk and process 1 minute on highest speed. Strain through 3 layers of cheesecloth into a pitcher. Makes 3 cups.

SAFFRON MILK

1 cup milk

¼ teaspoon saffron threads

1 cardamom pod

1 whole clove

1 (2- to 3-inch) cinnamon stick

2 tablespoons chopped unsalted almonds

1 tablespoon honey

Place 3 tablespoons milk in a small saucepan and heat until warm. Remove from heat, add saffron and let stand 10 minutes. Heat remaining milk in another saucepan until very warm. Add cardamom, clove, cinnamon stick and saffron-milk mixture. Stir, remove from heat and let stand 5 minutes. Strain into mug. Add almonds and honey; stir well. Makes 1 serving.

ORANGE ALMOND MILK

1½ cups unsalted roasted almonds

1⅔ cups powdered sugar

4 cups water

⅓ cup orange flower water

3 qts. milk (12 cups)

Drop almonds into a saucepan filled with boiling water and blanch 30 seconds. Drain almonds well, then rub in a towel to remove skins. Process almonds and ½ of powdered sugar in a blender until nuts are very finely ground. Combine almond mixture and water in a large bowl, cover and let stand overnight. Stir in orange flower water. Place milk in a large jug and add remaining powdered sugar. Strain almond mixture through cheesecloth into milk. Stir; refrigerate until well chilled. Makes 4 quarts.

MAPLE MILK

1 cup milk

1 tablespoon maple syrup

⅛ teaspoon ground coriander or ½ teaspoon chopped fresh cilantro (coriander)

Combine milk, maple syrup and coriander in a blender. Process 10 seconds on high speed. Makes 1 serving.

MILK & HONEY

1 qt. milk (4 cups)

3 tablespoons honey

Freshly grated nutmeg

Place milk in a saucepan and heat until very warm. Add honey and stir until dissolved. Sprinkle with nutmeg. Makes 4 servings.

ANGEL'S MILK

¼ cup peach nectar or ½ cup canned peach slices

½ cup milk

1 teaspoon almond extract

1 egg

2 ice cubes

Combine peach nectar or peach slices, milk, almond extract, egg and ice cubes in a blender. Process 10 seconds on high speed. Makes 1 serving.

DUTCH SPICED MILK

8 whole cloves

1 (2- to 3-inch) cinnamon stick

1 mace blade

¼ teaspoon saffron threads, if desired

1 qt. milk (4 cups)

2 tablespoons cornstarch

¼ cup water

½ cup sugar

Tie cloves, cinnamon stick, mace and, if desired, saffron together in a piece of cheesecloth. Put milk in a heavy saucepan. Add spice bag and heat until milk begins to bubble. Reduce heat to low, cover and simmer 30 minutes. Dissolve cornstarch in water in a small bowl. Add sugar and cornstarch mixture to milk. Simmer, stirring, 5 minutes. Discard spice bag. Makes 3 servings.

ANISE MILK

1 tablespoon anise seeds

1 qt. milk (4 cups)

½ cup sugar

2 tablespoons cornstarch

¼ cup water

Crush anise seeds in a mortar or bowl until powdered. Combine crushed anise seeds and milk in a saucepan and bring just to the boiling point over high heat. Immediately reduce heat to low. Add sugar, stir well and simmer 5 minutes. Dissolve cornstarch in water in a small bowl. Add to milk and cook, stirring, about 5 minutes or until mixture is slightly thickened. Makes 1 quart.

BUTTERSCOTCH STEAMER

½ gal. milk (2 qts.)

¼ cup unsalted butter

½ cup packed dark brown sugar

Ground cinnamon

Place milk in a saucepan and heat over low heat, stirring, until very warm. Add butter and stir until melted. Add brown sugar; stir until dissolved. Sprinkle with cinnamon. Makes 2 quarts.

ANGEL'S MILK

PEACH TANG

2 large ripe peaches
1 cup milk
¼ cup plain yogurt
2 teaspoons chopped walnuts

Peel, pit and coarsely chop peaches. Combine peaches, milk and yogurt in a blender. Process about 1 minute or until frothy. Garnish with walnuts. Makes 2 servings.

GINGER PEACHY

4 large ripe peaches
1 qt. milk (4 cups)
½ teaspoon ground ginger
2 tablespoons honey

Peel, pit and coarsely chop peaches. Combine peaches, milk, ginger and honey in a blender. Process about 1 minute or until frothy. Serve at once. Makes 6 servings.

DUTCH BANANA DRINK

1 pint milk (2 cups)
2 bananas, sliced
¼ cup whipping cream
2 tablespoons sugar
1 teaspoon lemon juice
1 egg yolk
Ice cubes

Combine milk, bananas, cream, sugar, lemon juice and egg yolk in a blender. Process about 45 seconds or until smooth. Serve over ice cubes. Makes 2 servings.

ORANGE MILK

1 cup milk
½ cup orange juice
2 tablespoons honey
1 egg
¼ teaspoon almond extract

Combine milk, orange juice, honey, egg and almond extract in a blender. Process about 1 minute or until smooth and thick. Makes 1 serving.

DATE DRINK

1 cup milk
8 oz. plain yogurt (1 cup)
4 ice cubes
12 dates, pitted and coarsely chopped
4 unsalted almonds

Combine milk, yogurt, ice cubes, dates and almonds in a blender. Process about 2 minutes or until smooth. Makes 2 servings.

FRUIT SMOOTHY

1 cup orange juice
1 cup crushed pineapple packed in unsweetened pineapple juice (about one 8-oz. can)
1 banana, sliced
1 cup milk
1 tablespoon honey
1 teaspoon pure vanilla extract
3 ice cubes
Mint sprigs

Combine orange juice, undrained pineapple, banana, milk, honey, vanilla and ice cubes in a blender. Process about 1 minute or until smooth. Garnish with mint sprigs. Makes 4 servings.

LEFT TO RIGHT: DUTCH BANANA DRINK, GINGER PEACHY, FRUIT SMOOTHY, DATE DRINK, ORANGE MILK

STRAWBERRY-BANANA MILK

2 bananas, sliced

¼ cup strawberry syrup

1 pint milk (2 cups)

Combine bananas, strawberry syrup amd milk in a blender. Process about 25 seconds or until smooth. Makes 2 servings.

PAPAYA-BANANA DRINK

2 bananas, sliced

2 eggs

2 ripe papayas, peeled, seeded and coarsely chopped

2 tablespoons honey

1 cup milk

¾ cup cold sparkling water

⅛ teaspoon freshly grated nutmeg

Combine bananas, eggs, papayas, honey and milk in a blender. Process about 1 minute or until smooth. Stir in sparkling water until frothy. Stir in nutmeg. Makes 2 servings.

CHOCOLATE-BANANA MILK

1 qt. milk (4 cups)

3 bananas, sliced

3 tablespoons unsweetened cocoa powder

3 tablespoons sugar

½ teaspoon ground cinnamon

Combine, milk, bananas, cocoa, sugar and cinnamon in a blender. Process about 1 minute or until smooth and frothy. Makes 4 servings.

INDIAN COCONUT MILK DRINK

1¾ cups milk

¼ cup cream of coconut

1 tablespoon whipping cream

2 tablespoons grated unsweetened coconut

6 unsalted pistachio nuts, shelled and coarsely chopped

Combine milk and cream of coconut in a blender. Process about 1 minute or until frothy. Pour into glasses; top each with some cream, coconut and pistachios. Makes 2 servings.

TROPICAL FROSTED

½ banana, sliced

½ cup milk

2 tablespoons unsweetened pineapple juice

1 teaspoon cream of coconut

½ cup crushed ice

Combine banana, milk, pineapple juice, cream of coconut and crushed ice in a blender. Process about 20 seconds or until smooth. Makes 1 serving.

PINEAPPLE MILK

6 tablespoons honey

3½ cups fresh pineapple cubes

3½ cups milk

1½ cups cracked ice

Combine honey, pineapple, milk and cracked ice in a blender. Process about 1 minute or until smooth. Makes 6 servings.

TROPICAL FROSTED

VANILLA-BANANA SHAKE

1 cup milk

1 banana, sliced

3 scoops vanilla ice cream, softened

1 teaspoon lemon juice

Freshly grated nutmeg

Combine milk, banana, ice cream and lemon juice in a blender. Process about 30 seconds or until smooth. Sprinkle with nutmeg. Makes 2 servings.

BANANA-DATE SHAKE

1 cup milk

1 tablespoon maple syrup

½ cup chopped dates

1 banana, sliced

8 oz. plain yogurt (1 cup)

½ teaspoon pure vanilla extract

Combine milk, maple syrup and dates in a blender. Process about 1 minute or until smooth. Add banana, yogurt and vanilla. Process about 30 seconds or until thick. Makes 2 servings.

CHOCOLATE-PEPPERMINT SHAKE

1/4 cup Chocolate Syrup, page 15, or purchased chocolate syrup

1 qt. vanilla ice cream, softened

1 pint milk (2 cups)

1/2 teaspoon peppermint extract

Whipped cream

2 tablespoons crushed peppermint candy

Combine Chocolate Syrup and 1/2 of ice cream in a blender. Process about 30 seconds or until smooth. Add milk and peppermint extract. Process about 30 seconds or until foamy. Top with scoops of remaining ice cream, whipped cream and crushed peppermint candy. Makes 4 servings.

PEACHY SHAKE

3 ripe peaches

1/2 cup honey

1 qt. milk (4 cups)

1/2 teaspoon almond extract

1 qt. vanilla ice cream, softened

Peel, pit and coarsely chop peaches. Combine peaches, honey and 2 cups milk in a blender. Process about 30 seconds or until smooth. Add remaining 2 cups milk, almond extract and 1/2 of ice cream. Process about 1 minute or until smooth. Top with scoops of remaining ice cream. Makes 6 servings.

BLUEBERRY FREEZE

1/4 cup fresh or frozen blueberries, thawed if frozen

3/4 cup pineapple sherbet, softened

2 tablespoons Blueberry Syrup, page 15, or purchased blueberry syrup

1/2 cup cold sparkling water

Set aside 6 blueberries. Combine remaining blueberries, sherbet, Blueberry Syrup and sparkling water in a blender. Process about 1 minute or until thick and smooth. Garnish with reserved blueberries. Makes 1 serving.

STRAWBERRY SHAKE

1/2 cup half and half

1/2 cup milk

1 cup strawberry ice cream, softened

1 tablespoon honey

1 cup fresh or frozen strawberries, thawed if frozen

2 tablespoons crushed ice

Whipped cream

Combine half and half, milk, ice cream, honey, strawberries and crushed ice in a blender. Process about 1 1/2 minutes or until smooth and thick. Top with whipped cream. Makes 2 servings.

CHOCOLATE-ORANGE SHAKE

3 cups milk

6 tablespoons Chocolate Syrup, page 15, or purchased chocolate syrup

1 qt. orange sherbet, softened

Whipped cream

Ground cinnamon

Combine 1 cup milk, 2 tablespoons Chocolate Syrup and 1/2 of sherbet in a blender. Process about 30 seconds or until smooth. Add remaining 2 cups milk and remaining 4 tablespoons Chocolate Syrup; process about 20 seconds or until frothy. Top with scoops of remaining sherbet and whipped cream; sprinkle with cinnamon. Makes 4 servings.

ORANGE-APRICOT SHAKE

2 1/2 cups milk

1 pint orange sherbet, softened

1/2 cup chopped dried apricots

2 tablespoons sugar

1/2 teaspoon pure vanilla extract

Combine 1 1/4 cups milk, 1/2 of sherbet, apricots, sugar and vanilla in a blender. Process about 1 minute or until smooth. Add remaining 1 1/4 cups milk and remaining sherbet. Process about 1 minute or until smooth and frothy. Serve immediately. Makes 4 servings.

MATTHA (Minted Indian Yogurt Drink)

8 oz. plain yogurt (1 cup)
¾ cup cold water
4 mint sprigs
½ teaspoon ground cumin
¼ teaspoon salt
8 ice cubes

Combine yogurt, water and 2 mint sprigs in a blender. Process about 30 seconds or until smooth..Add cumin, salt and ice cubes. Process about 30 seconds or until frothy. Serve immediately. Garnish each serving with 1 of the remaining mint sprigs. Makes 2 servings.

ROSE LASSI

SPARKLING YOGURT DRINK

64 oz. plain yogurt (8 cups)
5 cups cold sparkling water
Crushed ice

Line a colander with cheesecloth and fill with yogurt. Set colander in a bowl, cover and refrigerate 24 hours. Discard liquid in bowl. Place drained yogurt in bowl and beat with a whisk until creamy. Gradually beat in sparkling water. Pour into a large pitcher; fill pitcher with crushed ice. Makes 2½ quarts.

TIGER'S MILK

¾ cup plain yogurt
¾ cup orange juice
1 banana, sliced
3 tablespoons brewer's yeast
1 egg
2 tablespoons honey

Combine yogurt, orange juice, banana, yeast, egg and honey in a blender. Process about 30 seconds or until smooth. Serve immediately. Makes 2 servings.

HEALTH DRINK

8 oz. plain yogurt (1 cup)
1 tablespoon blackstrap molasses
1 teaspoon wheat germ

Combine yogurt, molasses and wheat germ in a blender. Process about 10 seconds or until smooth. Makes 1 serving.

ROSE LASSI

1½ cups plain yogurt
1 tablespoon rose water
3 tablespoons whipping cream
6 tablespoons sugar
10 ice cubes
Crushed ice

Combine yogurt, rose water, cream and sugar in a blender. Process about 30 seconds or until sugar is dissolved. Add ice cubes and process about 30 seconds or until frothy. Serve over crushed ice. Makes 2 servings.

LASSI (Indian Yogurt Drink)

8 oz. plain yogurt (1 cup)
1 cup water
⅛ teaspoon salt
⅛ teaspoon ground cumin
Crushed ice

Combine yogurt, water, salt and cumin in a blender. Process about 10 seconds or until smooth. Serve over crushed ice. Makes 2 servings.

FRUITY YOGURT DRINKS

FRUITY YOGURT DRINK

BLUEBERRY-YOGURT SHAKE

2 eggs
16 oz. plain yogurt (2 cups)
¼ cup blueberry preserves
1 cup milk
1 teaspoon bitters
Crushed ice

Combine eggs, yogurt, preserves, milk and bitters in a blender. Process about 30 seconds or until smooth. Serve over crushed ice. Makes 4 servings.

BANANA-YOGURT DRINK

½ cup plain yogurt
½ banana, sliced
1 teaspoon honey
½ teaspoon lemon juice
Lemon slice

Combine yogurt, banana, honey and lemon juice in a blender. Process about 20 seconds or until smooth. Garnish with lemon slice. Makes 1 serving.

APRICOT-YOGURT DRINK

½ cup plain yogurt
½ cup apricot nectar
½ teaspoon lemon juice
Mint sprig

Combine yogurt, apricot nectar and lemon juice in a blender. Process about 10 seconds or until smooth. Garnish with mint sprig. Makes 1 serving.

MINTY APPLE-YOGURT DRINK

½ cup plain yogurt
½ cup buttermilk
1 cup apple juice
2 mint sprigs
Apple slices

Combine yogurt, buttermilk, apple juice and mint sprigs in a blender. Process about 15 seconds or until smooth. Garnish with apple slices. Makes 2 servings.

PAPAYA-YOGURT DRINK

½ ripe papaya
½ cup plain yogurt
1 teaspoon honey
1 teaspoon lemon juice
Mint sprig

Peel, seed and coarsely chop papaya. Combine papaya, yogurt, honey and lemon juice in a blender. Process about 30 seconds or until smooth. Garnish with mint sprig. Makes 1 serving.

SUNNY YOGURT DRINK

½ cup plain yogurt
½ cup orange juice
¼ cup unsalted sunflower seeds, hulled

Combine yogurt, orange juice and sunflower seeds in a blender. Process about 1 minute or until smooth. Makes 1 serving.

FRUITY YOGURT DRINK

1 banana, sliced
8 oz. plain yogurt (1 cup)
1 cup orange juice
1 cup fresh strawberries, hulled
½ teaspoon pure vanilla extract
1 teaspoon honey

Set aside 3 banana slices. Combine remaining banana, yogurt, orange juice, strawberries, vanilla and honey in a blender. Process about 1 minute or until smooth. Garnish each serving with 1 of the reserved banana slices. Makes 3 servings.

LEMON-YOGURT DRINK

½ cup sliced fresh strawberries
1 tablespoon sugar
8 oz. lemon-flavored yogurt (1 cup)
¾ cup milk
2 fresh strawberries, hulled

Combine sliced strawberries, sugar, yogurt and milk in a blender. Process about 30 seconds or until frothy. Serve immediately. Garnish each serving with a strawberry. Makes 2 servings.

SPANISH MERINGUE MILK

1 qt. milk (4 cups)
1½ cups sugar
1 (1-inch) piece lemon peel
1 teaspoon lemon juice
1 (2- to 3-inch) cinnamon stick
4 egg whites
Ground cinnamon

Combine milk, 1 cup sugar, lemon peel, lemon juice and cinnamon stick in a saucepan. Simmer 5 minutes, stirring until sugar is dissolved. Remove from heat; cool. Strain into a bowl and place in freezer. In another bowl, beat egg whites and remaining ½ cup sugar until stiff. When milk begins to freeze, beat in meringue, a little at a time. Return to freezer and freeze about 1 hour or until firm. Fill glasses with frozen meringue milk; sprinkle with cinnamon. Serve with spoons. Makes 6 servings.

PEACH SOYMILK SHAKE

2 ripe peaches
1 teaspoon pure vanilla extract
2 tablespoons honey
1½ cups cold soymilk

Peel, pit and dice peaches. Combine peaches, vanilla, honey and soymilk in a blender. Process about 40 seconds or until smooth and frothy. Refrigerate until well chilled. Makes 2 servings.

RED BUTTERMILK

2 cups peeled, coarsely chopped beets
1 cup buttermilk
1 tablespoon lemon juice
Sugar to taste

Puree beets in a blender or a food processor fitted with a metal blade. Place a doubled cheesecloth square over a bowl. Pour puree into cloth; gather cloth around puree and twist to extract juice. Discard beets. Add buttermilk and lemon juice to beet juice in bowl; stir well. Sweeten with sugar and stir well. Refrigerate until well chilled. Makes 1 serving.

MANGO BUTTERMILK

1 cup peeled, diced ripe mango
½ cup buttermilk
1 teaspoon honey
½ teaspoon lemon juice
¼ teaspoon grated lemon peel
½ cup crushed ice
Mint sprig

Combine mango, buttermilk, honey, lemon juice, lemon peel and crushed ice in a blender. Process about 30 seconds or until smooth. Garnish with mint sprig. Makes 1 serving.

INDIAN BUTTERMILK DRINK

1 cup buttermilk
1 cup water
1 teaspoon honey
½ teaspoon rose water
Crushed ice

Combine buttermilk, water, honey and rose water in a bowl. Stir until smooth. Serve over crushed ice. Makes 2 servings.

TURKISH SEMOLINA DRINK

2½ cups milk
1 tablespoon semolina flour
1 tablespoon sugar
Ground cinnamon

Combine milk, semolina flour and sugar in a saucepan. Heat over low heat, stirring, 10 minutes. Sprinkle with cinnamon. Makes 2 servings.

BANANA-MAPLE SOY SHAKE

1 banana, sliced
1 cup cold soymilk
2 teaspoons lemon juice
1 tablespoon maple syrup
2 teaspoons wheat germ

Combine banana, soymilk, lemon juice, maple syrup and wheat germ in a blender. Process about 40 seconds or until smooth and frothy. Refrigerate until well chilled. Makes 1 serving.

MANGO BUTTERMILK

EGG FLIP

1 egg

1 teaspoon powdered sugar

⅔ cup milk

Freshly grated nutmeg

Break egg into glass. Add powdered sugar and beat well with a fork. Set aside. Place milk in a small saucepan and heat until very hot but not boiling. Slowly pour milk into glass while beating with fork. Pour flip back and forth from glass to saucepan until frothy. Sprinkle with nutmeg. Makes 1 serving.

BREAKFAST YOGURT EGGNOG

2 eggs, separated

1½ tablespoons sugar

1 cup milk

8 oz. plain yogurt (1 cup)

½ teaspoon pure vanilla extract

Freshly grated nutmeg

Place egg yolks and sugar in a bowl and beat until thick and lemon-colored. Add milk, yogurt and vanilla and stir well. In another bowl, using clean, dry beaters, beat egg whites until stiff. Fold into yogurt mixture. Sprinkle with nutmeg. Makes 4 servings.

CLASSIC EGGNOG

6 tablespoons sugar

6 eggs, separated

½ cup brandy

1 pint whipping cream (2 cups)

1½ qts. milk (6 cups)

Freshly grated nutmeg

Put 4 tablespoons sugar in a large bowl. Beat in egg yolks, 1 at a time, until mixture is thick and lemon-colored. Beat in brandy. Place egg whites and remaining 2 tablespoons sugar in another bowl. Using clean, dry beaters, beat until stiff. Set aside. Gradually and gently beat cream into egg-yolk mixture; then slowly beat in milk. Pour into glasses and top with meringue. Sprinkle with nutmeg. Makes 6 servings.

BANANA EGGNOG

1 egg
1 tablespoon maple syrup
1 banana, sliced
1 cup milk

Combine egg, maple syrup and banana in a blender. Process about 30 seconds or until smooth. Add milk and process 10 more seconds. Refrigerate until well chilled. Makes 1 serving.

HOT POSSET

1 pint milk (2 cups)
2 egg yolks
3 tablespoons honey
1 teaspoon grated lemon peel
1 cup apple cider
Freshly grated nutmeg

Combine milk, egg yolks, honey and lemon peel in top half of a double boiler over simmering water. Cook, stirring, until smooth and thickened. Stir in cider; cook, stirring, 1 minute. Sprinkle with nutmeg. Makes 2 servings.

EGGNOG FOR ONE

1 egg
1 cup milk
2 tablespoons whipping cream
½ teaspoon pure vanilla extract
Freshly grated nutmeg

Combine egg, milk, cream and vanilla in a blender. Process about 30 seconds or until smooth. Sprinkle with nutmeg. Makes 1 serving.

CLASSIC EGGNOG

Unusual Drinks

Many drinks that seem unusual to us, such as walnut tea and barley water, are familiar beverages in other parts of the world. Other drinks in this chapter qualify as "unusual" only because we aren't accustomed to thinking of them as drinks—broths and bouillons, for example. But remember that imagination, experimentation and an open mind are the foundations of good cooking—and good entertaining.

If you're not sure about the best way to serve a new and unusual drink, just let common sense be your guide. Serving hot drinks in cups or mugs is always acceptable, but why not be imaginative? Try presenting them in small, rimless bowls instead. Cold drinks can be served in any sort of glass; and a wine glass is always proper, no matter what the drink.

When should you serve a soup as a drink? In the days of the grand ocean liners, cups of beef bouillon were served to the passengers in the late morning. Today, few of us enjoy such luxury, but hot soups still make warming and satisfying beverages. There's no better way to chase away the chills after being outdoors on a cold day. A cup of soup, whether hot or cold, is also a good, nourishing alternative to beverages such as coffee or tea for a midmorning or midafternoon break.

Any soup served as a drink should be either a clear broth or a very smooth puree. There's no need to provide a spoon for soups served as beverages.

Certain unusual drinks are traditionally served in specific ways. Switchel, also sometimes called haying water, is a thirst-quenching beverage that in earlier days was often served to harvesters in the fields. Barley water is a traditional English drink that is still quite popular; it's often served to athletes at sporting events. You'll enjoy both barley water and switchel as refreshing drinks after exercise—both are just as thirst-quenching as some commercial drinks designed for athletes.

If you'd like to serve a drink for dessert, try zabaglione. This Italian favorite is a frothy, sweet concoction of eggs, cream and a touch of red wine. Serve it in a wine or parfait glass.

Even among unusual drinks, chocolate atole stands out. This thick, rich Mexican drink is made with masa harina (very finely ground cornmeal), cinnamon, brown sugar and chocolate. The flavor is a little different from what you might expect—try it.

If there's a peanut-butter-lover in your life, be sure to sample the West African peanut drink. This frothy and warming drink is definitely unusual and definitely delicious.

When you make these unusual drinks for the first time, follow the directions carefully—just as you would for a more familiar drink. After that, adapt the recipe to suit your personal taste.

VEGETABLE BOUILLON

WEST AFRICAN PEANUT DRINK

½ cup peanut butter
4 cups water
Salt to taste
1 tablespoon sugar

Place peanut butter in a saucepan. Very gradually stir in water. Bring to a boil over medium heat; then reduce heat and simmer 10 minutes. Add salt and sugar. Beat with a whisk until frothy. Serve hot. Makes 1 quart.

KOREAN WALNUT TEA

6 cups unsalted walnut halves
6 cups cold water
½ cup uncooked rice
2 cups sugar

Drop walnuts into a saucepan filled with boiling water and blanch 5 minutes. Drain walnuts well, then rub in a towel to remove skins. Chop walnuts coarsely and set aside. Place 3 cups cold water in a bowl, add rice and soak 15 minutes. Drain well, reserving liquid. Combine rice and walnuts in a food processor fitted with a metal blade. Process until smooth, gradually adding reserved rice liquid. Strain mixture through cheesecloth into a heavy saucepan. Squeeze to extract all liquid; discard solids remaining in cheesecloth. Add remaining 3 cups cold water and sugar to saucepan. Cook over medium heat, stirring constantly, 7 minutes. Makes 1½ quarts.

CHOCOLATE ATOLE

2½ cups water

½ cup masa harina (very finely ground cornmeal)

1½ oz. (1½ squares) semisweet chocolate, grated

1 (2- to 3-inch) cinnamon stick

1 tablespoon packed brown sugar

Place 1½ cups water in a saucepan and bring to a boil. Combine masa harina and remaining 1 cup water in a bowl. Mix well and pour into boiling water, stirring constantly until smooth. Add chocolate, cinnamon stick and brown sugar. Cook, stirring constantly, about 5 minutes or until mixture is thickened. Remove cinnamon stick and serve hot, with spoons. Makes 4 servings.

SPICED TOMATO BOUILLON

2½ cups canned whole tomatoes

1 onion, thinly sliced

1 teaspoon dried leaf oregano

½ teaspoon celery seeds

½ teaspoon black pepper

½ teaspoon salt

¼ teaspoon hot red-pepper flakes

2 cups beef broth

½ cup white wine

Combine tomatoes, onion, oregano, celery seeds, black pepper, salt and red-pepper flakes in a saucepan. Stir well. Cook over medium heat until bubbles form; reduce heat, cover and simmer 15 minutes. Combine broth and wine in a large saucepan. Heat over low heat until steaming; then strain tomato mixture into broth mixture. Heat until simmering. Serve hot. Makes 1 quart.

VEGETABLE BOUILLON

2 large carrots, chopped

2 large potatoes, diced

2 small onions, chopped

1 leek, chopped

2 celery stalks with leaves, chopped

2 zucchini, chopped

3 large ripe tomatoes, seeded and chopped

1 cup chopped green cabbage

1 cup chopped green beans

6 parsley sprigs

2 tablespoons chopped fresh basil or 1 teaspoon dried leaf basil

½ teaspoon dried leaf thyme

2 teaspoons salt

1 teaspoon pepper

3 qts. water (12 cups)

Combine all ingredients in a large pot. Bring to a boil over medium heat. Reduce heat to very low, cover and simmer 3 hours, stirring occasionally. Remove from heat; cool. Reheat and strain through cheesecloth into a soup tureen. Serve hot. Makes 3 quarts.

KOREAN WALNUT TEA

GAZPACHO

3 lbs. ripe tomatoes, seeded and coarsely chopped

1 onion, quartered

1 green bell pepper, coarsely chopped

½ cucumber, peeled, seeded and coarsely chopped

1 garlic clove, crushed

2 tablespoons red-wine vinegar

About 2 cups chicken broth

1 teaspoon salt

½ teaspoon black pepper

Chopped green onions

Chopped cucumber

Croutons

Combine tomatoes, quartered onion, bell pepper, cucumber and garlic in a blender or a food processor fitted with a metal blade. Process, in batches if necessary, until pureed. Pour into a large bowl and stir in vinegar, 2 cups broth, salt and black pepper. Cover and refrigerate 8 hours or overnight. Strain through a sieve into a large pitcher; thin with more broth if desired. Serve very cold, garnished with green onions, cucumber and croutons. Makes 2 quarts.

HORCHATA (South American Melon-Seed Drink)

2 cups fresh cantaloupe and/or watermelon and/ or pumpkin seeds

4 cups cold water

½ cup sugar

2 teaspoons ground cinnamon

Ice cubes

Rinse and drain melon seeds, then place in a blender. Process until finely ground. Combine ground melon seeds, water, sugar and cinnamon in a bowl; stir well. Refrigerate 3 hours. Strain through cheesecloth into a pitcher. Serve over ice cubes. Makes 1 quart.

LEMON BARLEY WATER

9 lemons

1 cup pearl barley

8 cups cold water

2 cups sugar

Cut peel from lemons in thin strips. Put peel in a large saucepan; set aside. Squeeze juice from lemons, then strain juice and set aside. Add barley and water to peel in saucepan and bring to a boil. Reduce heat, cover and simmer 20 minutes. Remove from heat; cool. Carefully pour liquid into a large pitcher; discard cooked barley and lemon peel in saucepan. Add lemon juice and sugar to pitcher; stir until sugar is dissolved. Refrigerate until well chilled. Makes 2 quarts.

ZABAGLIONE

½ cup half and half

4 egg yolks

4 teaspoons sugar

4 teaspoons red wine

½ cup crushed ice

Combine half and half, egg yolks, sugar, wine and crushed ice in a blender. Process on high speed about 1½ minutes or until frothy. Makes 2 servings.

SWITCHEL

4 cups hot water

1½ cups maple syrup

1 cup light molasses

1 teaspoon ground ginger

3 qts. ice water (12 cups)

Combine hot water, maple syrup, molasses and ginger in a 1-gallon jug. Stir until molasses is dissolved. Cool. Add ice water, stir well and refrigerate until well chilled. Makes 4 quarts.

LEMON BARLEY WATER

Punch

Originally, punch was a potent mixture with five ingredients—sugar, lime, water, rum and spices. In fact, the word "punch" comes from a Hindi word meaning "five." In former days, highly alcoholic punches were often made and drunk in huge quantities at lavish parties.

When it comes to quenching thirsts at a large gathering today, a big bowl of punch with little or no alcohol is still ideal. Quick and easy to make and serve, punch also leaves you free to enjoy your guests.

Most low alcohol and nonalcoholic punches are based on citrus or fruit juice, although tea is often used for less-sweet punches. Punches are typically sweetened and flavored with honey or sugar and spices; most include a carbonated liquid such as ginger ale or tonic water for fizz and sparkle. Pieces of fruit are almost always added.

Cold punches can usually be prepared in advance, with the sparkling liquid added just before serving. Always use ripe fruit, and cut it into small, manageable pieces. Chill the ingredients and combine them in the punch bowl; then add an ice block (see below).

Serve cold punch in an attractive large bowl—preferably one of clear glass, to show off the punch's color. The punch should be ladled from the bowl into punch cups, which generally hold 6 to 8 ounces (¾ to 1 cup). If you don't have punch cups, or if you have more guests than you have cups, wine glasses are perfectly acceptable.

Hot punches are best when prepared immediately before serving. Serve them in handled punch cups, mugs or teacups. Again, wine glasses are acceptable in a pinch.

Avoid using ice cubes in punches; they melt too quickly and dilute the drink. The best way to keep the punch cold is to use an ice block. Making a large ice block is easy—just use a ½-gallon milk or juice carton. Cut away the top of the carton, fill it three-quarters full with fresh water, and freeze it until solid. Then peel away the carton and add the ice block to the punch. Plastic bottles or storage containers also make handy molds for ice blocks; choose the size of container based on the amount of punch and the size of the punch bowl. For a more attractive ice block, fill a ring mold with water and freeze it. And for an ice block that won't dilute the drink at all, prepare and freeze some of the punch in advance.

No matter how you make the ice block, try adding pieces of fruit or maraschino cherries to the liquid before freezing. The increased visual appeal will add to the festivities.

CITRUS PUNCH

PUNCH FOR TEN

LIME PUNCH

1 cup lime juice
1 cup sugar
4 cups water
1 qt. cold sparkling water (4 cups)
2 limes, thinly sliced
Small ice block

Combine lime juice, sugar and water in a pitcher. Stir until sugar is dissolved. Refrigerate until well chilled. Pour into a punch bowl and add sparkling water and lime slices. Stir gently. Add ice block. Makes 2½ quarts.

DOUBLE GRAPE PUNCH

4 cups cold unsweetened grapefruit juice
4 cups cold grape juice
3 cups cold sparkling water
1 lemon, thinly sliced
Small ice block

Combine grapefruit juice, grape juice and sparkling water in a punch bowl. Stir well. Add lemon slices and ice block. Makes 3 quarts.

SPICED CRANBERRY PUNCH

½ cup sugar
1 cup water
6 whole cloves
3 (2- to 3-inch) cinnamon sticks
2 cups cold cranberry juice
1 cup cold orange juice
½ cup cold lemon juice
4 cups cold ginger ale
1 orange, thinly sliced
1 lemon, thinly sliced
Small ice block

Combine sugar, water, cloves and cinnamon sticks in a saucepan. Bring to a boil, stirring until sugar is dissolved. Reduce heat and simmer 5 minutes. Remove from heat; cool. Remove cloves and cinnamon sticks. Pour into a punch bowl. Add cranberry juice, orange juice, lemon juice and ginger ale. Stir gently. Add orange slices, lemon slices and ice block. Makes 2½ quarts.

LEFT TO RIGHT: SPICED CRANBERRY PUNCH, SPICED APPLE PUNCH, DOUBLE GRAPE PUNCH, RASPBERRY-LEMON PUNCH, PINK GRAPEFRUIT CUP

RASPBERRY-LEMON PUNCH

4 cups frozen raspberries, thawed

1½ cups water

½ cup honey

½ cup lemon juice

2 qts. cold sparkling water (8 cups)

1 lemon, thinly sliced

Small ice block

Puree raspberries with ½ cup water in a blender or a food processor fitted with a metal blade. Strain into a pitcher. Combine honey and remaining 1 cup water in a bowl; stir until honey is dissolved. Add to pitcher, then stir in lemon juice. Refrigerate until well chilled. Pour into a punch bowl and add sparkling water and lemon slices. Stir gently. Add ice block. Makes 3 quarts.

PINK GRAPEFRUIT CUP

4 pink grapefruit

2 cups orange juice

½ cup cranberry juice

6 tablespoons powdered sugar

4 cups cold ginger ale

1 banana, thinly sliced

10 maraschino cherries

Small ice block

Squeeze juice from grapefruit into a bowl, then strain into a pitcher. Add orange juice, cranberry juice and powdered sugar. Stir until sugar is dissolved. Refrigerate until well chilled. Pour into a punch bowl and add ginger ale, banana and maraschino cherries. Stir gently. Add ice block. Makes 2½ quarts.

SPICED APPLE PUNCH

⅓ cup sugar

3 cups cold water

3 (2- to 3-inch) cinnamon sticks

2½ cups cold apple cider

1 cup cold orange juice

½ cup cold lemon juice

Small ice block

Combine sugar, 1 cup water and cinnamon sticks in a saucepan. Bring to a boil, stirring until sugar is dissolved. Reduce heat and simmer 5 minutes. Remove from heat; cool. Remove cinnamon sticks. Pour into a punch bowl. Add remaining 2 cups water, cider, orange juice and lemon juice. Stir gently. Add ice block. Makes 2 quarts.

CITRUS PUNCH FOR FIFTY

2 (2- to 3-inch) cinnamon sticks
10 whole cloves
¾ cup sugar
2 cups water
2 cups honey
4 cups cold unsweetened grapefruit juice
8 cups cold orange juice
4 cups cold lemon juice
2 qts. cold sparkling water (8 cups)
1 orange, thinly sliced
1 lemon, thinly sliced
Large ice block

Combine cinnamon sticks, cloves, sugar and water in a saucepan. Bring to a boil, stirring until sugar is dissolved. Reduce heat and simmer 5 minutes. Add honey and stir until dissolved. Remove from heat; cool. Strain into a punch bowl. Add grapefruit juice, orange juice, lemon juice and sparkling water. Stir gently. Add orange slices, lemon slices and ice block. Makes 7 quarts.

FRUIT JUICE PUNCH

4 cups cold apricot nectar
4 cups cold cranberry juice
4 cups cold unsweetened grapefruit juice
4 cups cold unsweetened pineapple juice
1 orange, thinly sliced
Mint sprigs
Small ice block

Combine apricot nectar, cranberry juice, grapefruit juice and pineapple juice in a punch bowl. Stir gently. Add orange slices, mint sprigs and ice block. Makes 4 quarts.

ROSEMARY BRIDAL PUNCH

2 cups honey
4 cups water
2 cups cold lemon juice
3 tablespoons fresh rosemary leaves
8 cups sliced fresh strawberries
3 qts. cold water (12 cups)
2 cups cold lime juice
6 cups cold sparkling water
Large ice block
Rosemary sprigs

Combine honey, 4 cups water, ¼ cup lemon juice and rosemary leaves in a saucepan. Bring to a boil, stirring until honey is dissolved. Remove from heat and let stand 5 minutes. Strain into a large punch bowl. Press strawberries through a fine sieve into punch bowl. Add 3 quarts cold water, remaining 1¾ cups lemon juice, lime juice and sparkling water. Stir gently. Add ice block and rosemary sprigs. Makes 9 quarts.

TEA PUNCH

½ cup honey
½ cup sugar
4 cups hot strong tea
1 cup lemon juice
3 cups grape juice
2 cups orange juice
4 cups water
2 cups cold ginger ale
1 lemon, thinly sliced
Small ice block

Combine honey, sugar and tea in a large bowl. Stir until sugar is dissolved. Add lemon juice, grape juice, orange juice and water. Refrigerate until well chilled. Pour into a punch bowl; add ginger ale and lemon slices. Stir gently. Add ice block. Makes 4 quarts.

HOLIDAY PUNCH

3 thick slices fresh gingerroot
1 (2- to 3-inch) cinnamon stick
8 whole cloves
4 cardamom pods
1 gal. apple cider (4 qts.)
4 cups unsweetened pineapple juice
6 lemons, thinly sliced
6 oranges, thinly sliced
½ teaspoon salt
1½ cups rum, if desired

Tie gingerroot, cinnamon stick, cloves and cardamom together in a piece of cheesecloth. Combine cider, pineapple juice, lemon slices and orange slices in a large kettle or pot. Add spice bag and bring to a boil over low heat. Adjust heat and simmer 15 minutes, stirring. Stir in salt. Discard spice bag. Stir in rum just before serving, if desired. Serve hot. Makes 5 quarts.

ORANGE-BLOSSOM PUNCH

3 cups sugar
3 cups water
6 cups cold unsweetened grapefruit juice
6 cups cold orange juice
1½ cups cold lime juice
3 tablespoons orange flower water
6 cups cold ginger ale
1 orange, thinly sliced
Large ice block

Combine sugar and water in a saucepan. Bring to a boil, stirring until sugar is dissolved. Reduce heat and simmer 5 minutes. Remove from heat; cool. Pour into a punch bowl. Add grapefruit juice, orange juice, lime juice, orange flower water and ginger ale. Stir gently. Add orange slices and ice block. Makes 6 quarts.

ROSEMARY BRIDAL PUNCH

Wine

As more and more Americans turn away from hard liquor, wine and wine-based drinks are growing rapidly in popularity. Commercial wine coolers (made with wine, fruit flavorings and sparkling water), for example, have been a hit with consumers. In addition, a number of low-alcohol and nonalcoholic wines are now available. These beverages have all the sophisticated flavor of wine, without the alcohol—and without the calories.

One of the best things about wine-based drinks is that they're good-tasting even when made with inexpensive jug wines. Save your special bottles for serving with special meals.

Serving wine. Every wine has an optimal serving temperature. *Red wines* should be served at about 60°F (15°C) to 65°F (20°C)—room temperature in the days before central heating. Most red wines and rosés can also be served slightly chilled; half an hour in the refrigerator is usually enough. *White wines* are best when served chilled. Put them in the refrigerator for about 2 hours before serving, or chill the bottles about 20 minutes in an ice-filled wine cooler. (If the wine is to be used in a drink with ice, it is preferable but not necessary to chill it first.) *Sparkling wines* taste best when cool, not icy cold. Refrigerate the bottles about an hour before serving. *Sherry* should not be chilled.

Count on approximately six servings for every 750-milliliter bottle of red, white or sparkling wine.

Wine served "straight" should always be sipped from a wine glass; sparkling wine can also be served in a champagne flute. Serve wine-based drinks such as coolers and spritzers either in wine glasses or in regular tall glasses.

When serving wine by itself, never fill the wine glass more than half full—the empty space allows the aroma of the wine to blossom. On a hot day, it is perfectly acceptable to add a few ice cubes to a glass of white wine.

Opening sparkling wine. To open a bottle of sparkling wine, hold the bottle at a 45-degree angle. Remove the wire around the cork. Hold the bottle firmly in one hand and grasp the cork with the other. Slowly twist the bottle, not the cork, until the cork eases out with a pop. To serve the wine, pour some into the glass until the foam almost reaches the rim. Wait a moment while the foam subsides, then fill the glass two-thirds full.

Storing wine. Unopened bottles of wine should be stored on their sides in a cool, dry, dark place. After opening the bottle, use the wine quickly. Opened red wines can be stored at room temperature for a few days; white wines will keep in the refrigerator for the same time. All opened jug wines should be stored in the refrigerator. Never store an opened bottle of sparkling wine; it will become flat very quickly.

WHITE WINE SPRITZER

Ice cubes
½ cup cold white wine
½ cup cold sparkling water
Lemon twist

Fill glass with ice cubes. Add wine and sparkling water, stir gently. Garnish with lemon twist. Makes 1 Serving.

WATERMELON COOLER

Ice cubes
¾ cup cubed, seeded watermelon
½ cup cold dry white wine
½ teaspoon Grenadine syrup
½ cup crushed ice

Fill glass with ice cubes. Set aside 1 watermelon cube. Combine remaining watermelon, wine, Grenadine syrup and crushed ice in a blender. Process on low speed 15 seconds. Pour into glass. Garnish with reserved watermelon cube. Makes 1 serving.

SPIKED CITRUS COOLER

Ice cubes
2 tablespoons vodka
2 teaspoons Grenadine syrup
2 teaspoons lemon juice
¼ teaspoon pure vanilla extract
6 tablespoons cold white wine

Fill glass with ice cubes. Add vodka, Grenadine syrup, lemon juice and vanilla; stir. Add wine and stir again. Makes 1 serving.

LEMON COOLER

Ice cubes
¼ cup cold white wine
1 teaspoon lemon juice
6 tablespoons cold lemon-flavored soda
Lemon twist

Fill glass with ice cubes. Add wine, lemon juice and lemon-flavored soda; stir. Garnish with lemon twist. Makes 1 serving.

LEFT TO RIGHT: SPIKED CITRUS COOLER, V
SPRITZER, KIR, LEMON COOLER, WATERM

KIR SHERBET

2 tablespoons crème de cassis or raspberry syrup

½ cup cold white wine

¼ cup crushed ice

Combine crème de cassis or raspberry syrup, wine and crushed ice in a blender. Process about 15 seconds or until smooth. Pour into glass. Makes 1 serving.

CRANBERRY SPRITZER

Ice cubes

6 tablespoons cranberry juice

¼ cup apple cider

6 tablespoons cold white wine

Cold sparkling water

Fill glass with ice cubes. Add cranberry juice, cider and wine. Stir. Fill glass with sparkling water. Makes 1 serving.

FROZEN COOLER

6 tablespoons cold white wine

2 teaspoons Triple Sec or Cointreau

1 teaspoon lemon juice

½ teaspoon almond extract

1 cup crushed ice

Orange slice

Combine wine, Triple Sec or Cointreau, lemon juice, almond extract and ½ cup crushed ice in a blender. Process on low speed about 10 seconds or until smooth. Put remaining ½ cup crushed ice in glass. Strain mixture into glass. Garnish with orange slice. Makes 1 serving.

PINEAPPLE COOLER

Ice cubes

¼ cup unsweetened pineapple juice

½ teaspoon superfine sugar

6 tablespoons cold white wine

6 tablespoons cold sparkling water

Peel of 1 lemon, cut in a spiral

Fill glass with ice cubes. Add pineapple juice, sugar and wine. Stir. Add sparkling water. Add lemon peel, dangling end over rim of glass. Makes 1 serving.

KIR

2 teaspoons crème de cassis or raspberry syrup

6 tablespoons cold white wine

Pour crème de cassis or raspberry syrup into glass. Add wine and stir gently. Makes 1 serving.

CRANBERRY SPARKLER

ORANGE FIZZ

Peel of ½ orange, cut in a spiral

1 teaspoon Triple Sec or Cointreau

½ cup cold sparkling wine

Place orange peel in glass. Add Triple Sec or Cointreau. Add sparkling wine and stir gently. Makes 1 serving.

BLUEBERRY BOUNCE

6 tablespoons cold sparkling wine

2 tablespoons Grenadine syrup

¼ cup cold sparkling water

4 fresh blueberries

Pour sparkling wine into glass. Add Grenadine syrup and sparkling water. Drop blueberries into drink. Blueberries will float up and down. Makes 1 serving.

LONDON SPECIAL

1 sugar cube

¼ teaspoon bitters

Ice cubes

½ cup cold sparkling wine

Orange twist

Place sugar cube in glass. Sprinkle with bitters. Fill glass with ice cubes and add sparkling wine. Stir gently. Garnish with orange twist. Makes 1 serving.

MIMOSA

6 tablespoons orange juice

10 tablespoons cold sparkling wine

Pour orange juice into glass. Stir in sparkling wine. Makes 1 serving.

KIR ROYALE

2 teaspoons crème de cassis or raspberry syrup

6 tablespoons cold sparkling wine

Pour crème de cassis or raspberry syrup into glass. Add 2 tablespoons sparkling wine and stir gently. Add remaining 4 tablespoons sparkling wine. Makes 1 serving.

GRENADINE TINGLER

1 teaspoon Grenadine syrup

½ cup cold sparkling wine

Pour Grenadine syrup into glass. Add sparkling wine and stir gently. Makes 1 serving.

SPINNING PEACH

1 small ripe peach

¾ cup cold sparkling wine

Rub peach gently all over with a paper towel to remove fuzz. Pierce surface 15 times with a fork. Place peach in glass and add sparkling wine. Peach will float and spin in glass. Makes 1 serving.

PEACH SPARKLER

½ cup fresh or canned peach slices

¼ teaspoon lemon juice

¼ teaspoon Grenadine syrup

1 teaspoon superfine sugar

Ice cubes

¾ cup cold sparkling wine

Puree peach slices and lemon juice in a blender. Add Grenadine syrup and sugar; process 5 seconds. Fill glass with ice cubes. Add peach puree and sparkling wine. Stir gently. Makes 1 serving.

FRUITY COOLER

Ice cubes

2 tablespoons cranberry juice

1 tablespoon grape juice

1 tablespoon raspberry syrup or crème de cassis

¼ cup cold dry red wine

Fill glass with ice cubes. Add cranberry juice, grape juice, raspberry syrup or crème de cassis and wine. Stir well. Makes 1 serving.

RED WINE FRAPPÉ

¾ cup crushed ice

½ cup cold dry red wine

1 teaspoon crème de cassis or raspberry syrup

Lemon twist

Place crushed ice in glass. Pour wine slowly over ice. Add crème de cassis or raspberry syrup. Garnish with lemon twist. Makes 1 serving.

RED WINE FLIP

6 tablespoons cold rosé wine

1½ tablespoons lime juice

1 teaspoon superfine sugar

Ice cubes

Lime slice

Combine wine, lime juice and sugar in a cocktail shaker with ice cubes. Shake well. Strain into glass. Garnish with lime slice. Makes 1 serving.

PURPLE ROSÉ

Ice cubes

6 tablespoons cold dry red wine

1 egg

1 teaspoon superfine sugar

Freshly grated nutmeg

Fill glass with ice cubes. Combine wine, egg and sugar in a cocktail shaker with ice cubes. Shake well and strain into glass. Sprinkle with nutmeg. Makes 1 serving.

ROSÉ DAIQUIRI

Ice cubes

6 tablespoons cold rosé wine

6 tablespoons prune juice

¼ cup cold sparkling water

Lemon slice

Fill glass with ice cubes. Add wine and prune juice. Stir. Add sparkling water; stir gently. Garnish with lemon slice. Makes 1 serving.

RED WINE COOLER

Ice cubes
½ cup cold dry red wine
2 tablespoons orange juice
2 teaspoons lemon juice
6 tablespoons cold sparkling water
2 tablespoons brandy, if desired
Peel of 1 orange, cut in a spiral
Lemon twist

Fill glass with ice cubes. Add wine, orange juice, lemon juice, sparkling water and brandy, if desired. Drop orange peel into glass. Garnish with lemon twist. Makes 1 serving.

RED WINE COBBLER

1 teaspoon superfine sugar
1 teaspoon lemon juice
¼ teaspoon Grenadine syrup
Crushed ice
¾ cup cold dry red wine
Pineapple spear

Combine sugar, lemon juice and Grenadine syrup in glass. Stir. Fill glass with crushed ice. Add wine; stir. Garnish with pineapple spear. Makes 1 serving.

ROSÉ DAIQUIRI

HOT TUB

1 (750-ml.) bottle dry red wine

½ cup honey

1 teaspoon ground cloves

4 orange slices

4 (2- to 3-inch) cinnamon sticks

Place wine in a saucepan and heat over low heat; do not allow to boil. Remove from heat, add honey and stir until dissolved. Add cloves; stir again. Pour into mugs. Garnish each serving with 1 orange slice and 1 cinnamon stick. Makes 4 servings.

HOT LEMON WINE

HOT BUTTERED WINE

½ cup dry red wine
¼ cup hot water
1 teaspoon unsalted butter
2 teaspoons maple syrup
Freshly grated nutmeg

Place wine in a small saucepan and heat until steaming. Add water and heat until mixture just at the boiling point. Pour into mug; add butter and maple syrup. Stir and sprinkle with nutmeg. Serve immediately. Makes 1 serving.

GLOW WINE

¾ cup dry red wine
1½ teaspoons superfine sugar
1 (2- to 3-inch) cinnamon stick
1 whole clove
1 teaspoon rum

Combine wine, sugar, cinnamon stick and clove in a small saucepan. Bring to a boil over low heat. Remove cinnamon stick and clove and pour into mug. Top with rum. Makes 1 serving.

HOT LEMON WINE

6 tablespoons dry red wine
3 tablespoons lemon juice
1½ teaspoons superfine sugar
6 tablespoons boiling water
Lemon twist

Combine wine, lemon juice and sugar in mug. Stir until sugar is dissolved. Add water; stir well. Garnish with lemon twist. Makes 1 serving.

HOT SPICED WINE

4 cups dry red wine
⅔ cup sugar
1 apple, cored and quartered
1 orange, quartered
3 dried figs, halved
6 unsalted almonds
1 (2- to 3-inch) cinnamon stick
3 whole cloves
¼ cup brandy

Combine wine, sugar, apple, orange, figs, almonds, cinnamon stick and cloves in a large saucepan. Heat over high heat 12 minutes, stirring until sugar is dissolved. Remove from heat, cover and let stand 5 minutes. Stir in brandy. Strain into mugs. Makes 1 quart.

HOT MULLED WINE

1 teaspoon superfine sugar
¼ cup water
10 tablespoons dry red wine
1½ teaspoons lemon juice
¼ teaspoon orange bitters
¼ teaspoon ground cinnamon

Combine sugar and water in a small saucepan. Heat over low heat, stirring, until sugar is dissolved. Remove from heat and add wine, lemon juice, bitters and cinnamon. Stir and pour into mug. Carefully heat a metal skewer over stove burner. Holding skewer in a potholder, insert into drink and stir. Makes 1 serving.

DRY WHITE SANGRIA

1 (750-ml.) bottle cold dry white wine
2 cups cold sparkling water
3 tablespoons lemon juice
3 tablespoons brandy
Peel of 1 lemon, cut in a spiral
½ cucumber, peeled and sliced
Ice cubes

Combine wine, sparkling water, lemon juice, brandy, lemon peel and cucumber in a large pitcher. Stir gently. Fill pitcher with ice cubes. Makes 6 servings.

RED WINE SANGRIA

3 small ripe peaches
1 (750-ml.) bottle cold dry red wine
½ cup Triple Sec or Cointreau
1 orange, thinly sliced
1 lemon, thinly sliced
2 cups cold sparkling water
Ice cubes

Peel, pit and dice peaches. Combine peaches, wine, Triple Sec or Cointreau, orange slices and lemon slices in a large pitcher. Add sparkling water; stir gently. Fill pitcher with ice cubes. Makes 6 servings.

SANGRIA CALIFORNIA

½ cup cold lemon juice
1 cup cold orange juice
2 tablespoons sugar
2 cups cold white grape juice
1 lemon, thinly sliced
1 orange, thinly sliced
Ice cubes
3 cups cold sparkling water

Combine lemon juice, orange juice and sugar in a large pitcher. Stir until sugar is dissolved. Add grape juice, lemon slices and orange slices; stir. Fill pitcher with ice cubes and add sparkling water. Stir gently. Makes 6 servings.

SWEET WHITE SANGRIA

1 (750-ml.) bottle cold dry white wine

2 cups cold ginger ale

3 tablespoons lemon juice

3 tablespoons Triple Sec or Cointreau

1 (2- to 3-inch) cinnamon stick

1 apple, peeled, cored and coarsely chopped

1 orange, thinly sliced

Ice cubes

Combine wine, ginger ale, lemon juice, Triple Sec or Cointreau, cinnamon stick, apple and orange slices in a large pitcher. Stir gently. Fill pitcher with ice cubes. Makes 6 servings.

RED WINE SANGRIA

HOT SHERRY TODDY

2 teaspoons honey

¼ cup dry sherry

½ cup boiling water

Freshly grated nutmeg

1 (2- to 3-inch) cinnamon stick

Place honey in mug. Add sherry and water; stir until honey is dissolved. Sprinkle with nutmeg and garnish with cinnamon stick. Makes 1 serving.

FARMER'S DAUGHTER

1 egg, separated

1 tablespoon superfine sugar

2 tablespoons dry sherry

⅛ teaspoon cinnamon

Place egg yolk and sugar in a small bowl and beat until creamy. Slowly beat in sherry. Set aside. In another small bowl, using clean, dry beaters, beat egg white until soft peaks form. Stir egg-yolk mixture into egg white until well blended. Spoon into glass and sprinkle with cinnamon. Serve with a spoon. Makes 1 serving.

ORANGE VELVET

¾ cup orange juice
¼ cup lime juice
1 cup sweet sherry
2 teaspoons sugar
1 egg white
6 ice cubes

Combine orange juice, lime juice, sherry, sugar, egg white and ice cubes in a blender. Process about 20 seconds or until smooth and frothy. Makes 2 servings.

MILKMAID

2 tablespoons dry sherry
2 tablespoons orange juice
1 teaspoon brandy
2 teaspoons whipping cream
6 tablespoons crushed ice

Combine sherry, orange juice, brandy, cream and crushed ice in a cocktail shaker. Shake well and strain into glass. Makes 1 serving.

IBIZA

Ice cubes
2 tablespoons dry sherry
⅛ teaspoon pure vanilla extract
1 tablespoon Triple Sec or Cointreau
½ cup cold tonic water

Fill glass with ice cubes. Add sherry, vanilla and Triple Sec or Cointreau; stir. Add tonic water. Makes 1 serving.

LEFT TO RIGHT: ORANGE VELVET, HOT SHERRY TODDY, IBIZA, MILKMAID, SHERRY FRUIT PITCHER SERVING

MINCE • GRATE • BLEND • SHRED • GRIND
BEAT • PUREE • CREAM • CHOP
OUNCE .045 LITER
OUNCE .030 LITER
OUNCE .015 LITER

Mixed Drinks

The sophisticated taste and relaxing effect of a mixed drink doesn't have to depend on alcohol. Today, more and more guests request low-alcohol and nonalcoholic cocktails—drinks that usually contain less than an ounce of a liqueur or apéritif wine. Sometimes called "mocktails," these drinks rarely contain hard liquor.

There are literally thousands of recipes for cocktails with and without alcohol, and more are invented every day. The recipes in this chapter present just a sampling of both classic favorites and recent developments.

Mixing a drink. A mixed drink is a careful blend of flavors—too much or too little of an ingredient will distort the taste. Always measure the ingredients accurately. Never multiply the ingredients to make more than one drink; instead, mix each drink separately. Many mixed drinks can be made directly in the serving glass, but some must be mixed in a cocktail shaker or processed in a blender to achieve a smooth consistency.

Using a cocktail shaker. A cocktail shaker is generally used when a drink must be mixed and chilled but served without ice. Place the drink ingredients in the shaker and add the ice (cubes, cracked ice or crushed ice, according to the recipe). The more ice you add, the faster the drink will get cold—but if you use too much ice, you'll prevent the ingredients from blending together. Cover the shaker securely, grasp one end in each hand and shake it up and down with authority. You will quickly feel the shaker get icy cold—the drink is ready at this point. Don't overshake or the drink will be diluted by the melting ice. Remove the cover, hold a coil-rimmed strainer against the shaker, and pour the drink into the glass. Serve at once.

Serving mixed drinks. Somehow, a mixed drink always tastes better when it nearly fills the glass. If the drink recipe makes a 6-ounce (3/4-cup) drink, for example, try to serve it in a glass close to that capacity. However, a wine glass is an excellent alternative for any drink. Thoughtful hosts provide a small napkin along with the drink.

Garnishes. A garnish adds the final elegant touch to a mixed drink—no mixed drink should be served without one! Try a slice of citrus fruit, a fresh strawberry, a pineapple cube, a maraschino cherry—use your imagination.

Many drink recipes call for a citrus twist. This is a strip of fresh citrus peel, 2 to 3 inches long and 1/4 inch wide, shaved just from the colored part of the rind; there should be no white pith on it. Twist the peel over the drink to release the fragrant oils, then drop it into the drink. The twist adds a subtle flavor that's an important part of the drink, so don't leave it out even if other garnishes are added.

AMELIA

Ice cubes

10 canned pineapple cubes, drained

¼ cup orange juice

2 tablespoons blackberry syrup or crème de cassis

Fill glass with ice cubes. Reserve 1 pineapple cube; combine remaining pineapple cubes, orange juice and 2 ice cubes in a blender. Process about 10 seconds or until smooth. Pour into glass. Float blackberry syrup or crème de cassis on top. Garnish with reserved pineapple cube; serve with a straw. Makes 1 serving.

APPLE PIE

2 tablespoons sweet vermouth

6 tablespoons apple juice

1 tablespoon lime juice

4 ice cubes

Cold sparkling water

Apple slice

Combine vermouth, apple juice, lime juice and ice cubes in a blender. Process about 15 seconds or until smooth. Pour into glass; fill glass with sparkling water. Garnish with apple slice. Makes 1 serving.

LEFT TO RIGHT: AMELIA, AMERICANO, ABBOT, APPLE PIE, BANANA PASSION

ALMOND BLOSSOM

1 tablespoon lemon juice
¼ cup plain yogurt
1 tablespoon honey
¼ teaspoon almond extract
6 tablespoons pear nectar
¾ cup cold sparkling water
Pear slice

Combine lemon juice, yogurt, honey, almond extract and pear nectar in a blender. Process about 10 seconds or until smooth. Refrigerate until well chilled. Pour into glass; add sparkling water. Stir gently and garnish with pear slice. Makes 1 serving.

BANANA PASSION

1 banana, sliced
2 tablespoons half and half
¼ cup passion-fruit nectar
4 ice cubes

Reserve 1 banana slice. Combine remaining banana, half and half, passion-fruit nectar and ice cubes in a blender. Process about 15 seconds or until smooth. Garnish with reserved banana slice. Makes 1 serving.

AMERICANO

Ice cubes
¼ cup sweet vermouth
¼ cup Campari apéritif wine
Cold sparkling water
Lemon twist

Fill glass with ice cubes. Add vermouth and Campari. Fill with sparkling water; stir. Garnish with lemon twist. Makes 1 serving.

ABBOT

3 tablespoons Frangelico liqueur
¼ banana, sliced
¼ cup unsweetened pineapple juice
6 tablespoons crushed ice
2 dashes bitters
2 hazelnuts, crushed

Combine Frangelico, banana, pineapple juice, crushed ice and bitters in a blender. Process about 20 seconds or until smooth. Garnish with hazelnuts. Makes 1 serving.

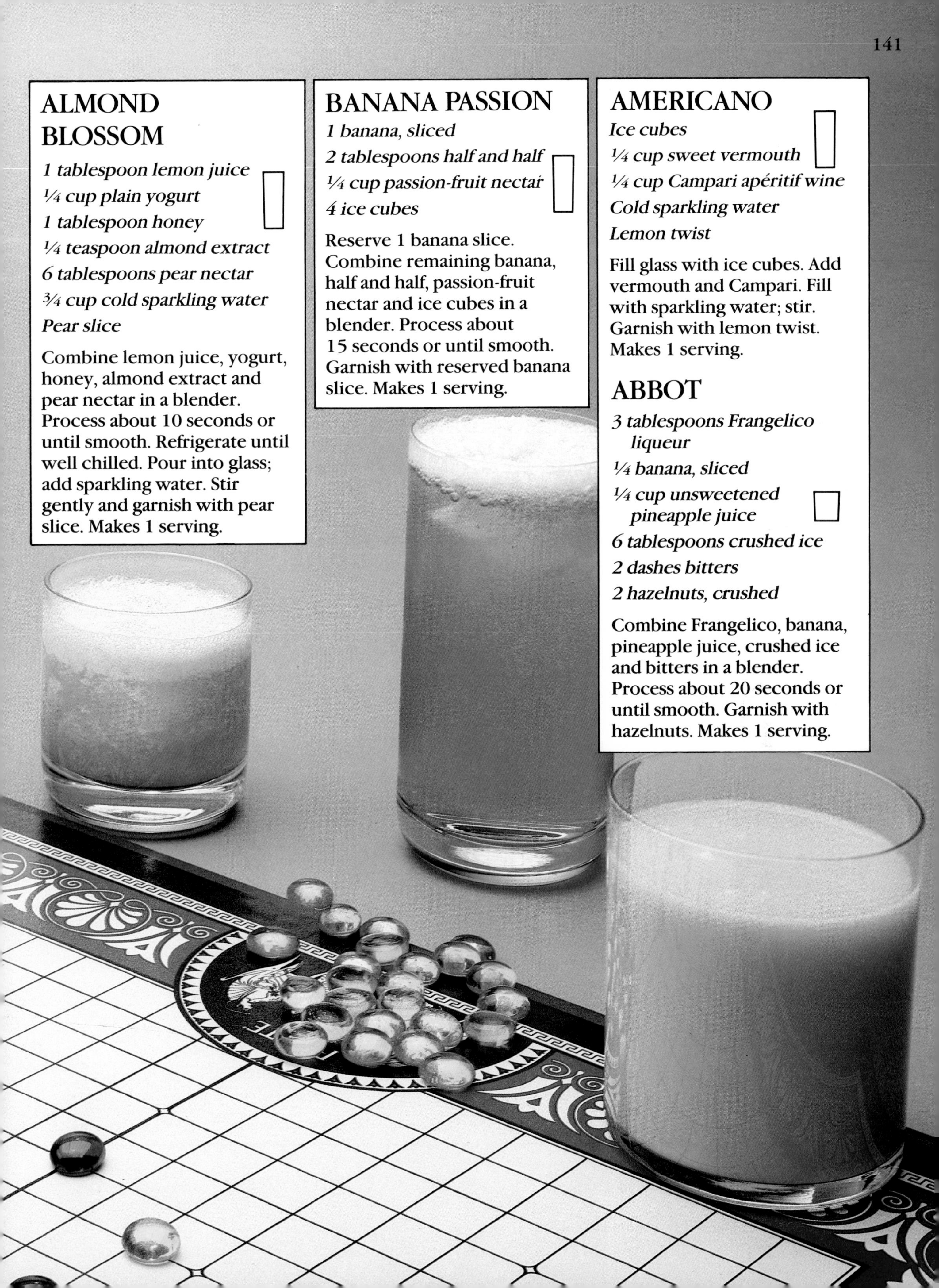

COCOMINT

1 tablespoon peppermint schnapps

¼ cup unsweetened grapefruit juice

¼ cup unsweetened pineapple juice

2 tablespoons cream of coconut

Ice cubes

Pineapple spear

Fill glass with ice cubes. Combine grapefruit juice, pineapple juice, cream of coconut and schnapps in a blender. Process 5 seconds. Pour into glass. Garnish with pineapple spear. Makes 1 serving.

CLUB COCKTAIL

1 sugar cube

2 dashes bitters

1 (2-inch-long) lemon twist

Ice cubes

Cold sparkling water

Put sugar cube in glass and splash with bitters. Add lemon twist; fill glass with ice cubes. Add sparkling water to fill. Makes 1 serving.

COUNTRY-CLUB COOLER

½ teaspoon Grenadine syrup

¾ cup cold sparkling water

Ice cubes

¼ cup dry vermouth

Peel of 1 orange, cut in a spiral

Peel of 1 lemon, cut in a spiral

Combine Grenadine syrup and ¼ cup sparkling water in glass; stir. Fill glass with ice cubes. Add vermouth and remaining ½ cup sparkling water; stir. Add orange peel and lemon peel, dangling ends over rim of glass. Makes 1 serving.

LEFT TO RIGHT: CRANBERRY COCKTAIL, COCOMINT, CLUB COCKTAIL, BOCCIE BALL, COUNTRY-CLUB COOLER, BITTERS HIGHBALL

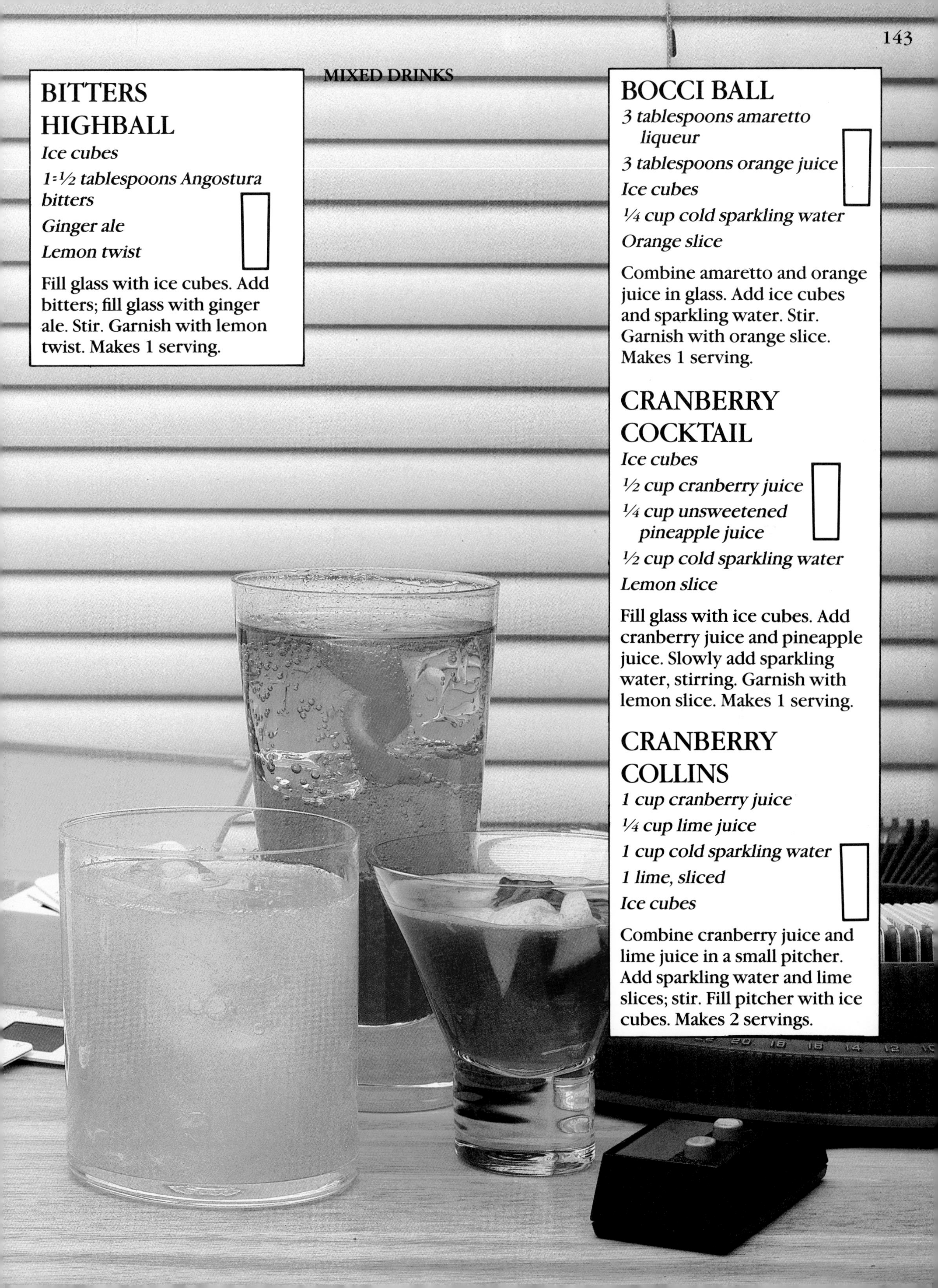

BITTERS HIGHBALL

Ice cubes

1-½ tablespoons Angostura bitters

Ginger ale

Lemon twist

Fill glass with ice cubes. Add bitters; fill glass with ginger ale. Stir. Garnish with lemon twist. Makes 1 serving.

BOCCI BALL

3 tablespoons amaretto liqueur

3 tablespoons orange juice

Ice cubes

¼ cup cold sparkling water

Orange slice

Combine amaretto and orange juice in glass. Add ice cubes and sparkling water. Stir. Garnish with orange slice. Makes 1 serving.

CRANBERRY COCKTAIL

Ice cubes

½ cup cranberry juice

¼ cup unsweetened pineapple juice

½ cup cold sparkling water

Lemon slice

Fill glass with ice cubes. Add cranberry juice and pineapple juice. Slowly add sparkling water, stirring. Garnish with lemon slice. Makes 1 serving.

CRANBERRY COLLINS

1 cup cranberry juice

¼ cup lime juice

1 cup cold sparkling water

1 lime, sliced

Ice cubes

Combine cranberry juice and lime juice in a small pitcher. Add sparkling water and lime slices; stir. Fill pitcher with ice cubes. Makes 2 servings.

CUBA ALCOHOL-LIBRE

Ice cubes
1 tablespoon lime juice
¾ cup cola soda
Lime slice

Fill glass with ice cubes. Add lime juice. Add cola; stir. Garnish with lime slice. Makes 1 serving.

DUKE COCKTAIL

1 tablespoon Triple Sec or Cointreau
2 teaspoons orange juice
1 tablespoon lemon juice
½ teaspoon Grenadine syrup
1 egg
Ice cubes
½ cup cold sparkling water
Orange slice

Combine Triple Sec or Cointreau, orange juice, lemon juice, Grenadine syrup and egg in a cocktail shaker with ice cubes. Shake well and strain into glass. Add sparkling water; stir. Garnish with orange slice. Makes 1 serving.

DUBONNET FIZZ

Ice cubes
3 tablespoons orange juice
1 tablespoon lemon juice
1 teaspoon Grenadine syrup
¼ cup Dubonnet apéritif wine
Cold sparkling water
Lemon twist

Fill glass with ice cubes. Combine orange juice, lemon juice, Grenadine syrup and Dubonnet in a cocktail shaker with ice cubes. Shake well and strain into glass. Fill glass with sparkling water; stir. Garnish with lemon twist. Makes 1 serving.

DUBONNET HIGHBALL

Ice cubes
¼ cup Dubonnet apéritif wine
Ginger ale
Lemon twist

Fill glass with ice cubes. Add Dubonnet. Fill glass with ginger ale; stir. Garnish with lemon twist. Makes 1 serving.

GINGERAPPLE

2 cups apple cider
2 tablespoons finely chopped crystallized ginger
2 teaspoons Grenadine syrup
Apple slices

Combine cider, ginger and Grenadine syrup in a blender. Process about 15 seconds or until smooth. Garnish with apple slices. Makes 2 servings.

GRAPE FOLLY

Ice cubes
6 tablespoons white grape juice
6 tablespoons cold sparkling water
1 tablespoon lime juice
Lime slice

Fill glass with ice cubes. Add grape juice, then sparkling water. Add lime juice; stir gently. Garnish with lime slice. Makes 1 serving.

LEFT TO RIGHT: DUBONNET FIZZ, DUBONNET HIGHBALL

PIATTI da FARSI (cont.)
Fagiano Arrosto
CONTORNI
FORMAGGI

GRENADINE RICKEY

Ice cubes

2 tablespoons lime juice

3 tablespoons Grenadine syrup

Cold sparkling water

Lime wedge

Fill glass with ice cubes. Add lime juice and Grenadine syrup. Fill glass with sparkling water. Stir. Drop lime wedge into glass. Makes 1 serving.

GREEN APPLE COCKTAIL

½ cup apple cider

¼ cup ginger ale

1 tablespoon lime juice

Ice cubes

Lime slice

Combine cider, ginger ale and lime juice in glass. Stir gently. Fill glass with ice cubes. Garnish with lime slice. Makes 1 serving.

ISLAND ORANGE

2 cups orange juice

½ teaspoon grated orange peel

¼ cup cream of coconut

1 tablespoon Grenadine syrup

6 ice cubes

Orange slices

Combine orange juice, orange peel, cream of coconut, Grenadine syrup and ice cubes in a blender. Process about 20 seconds or until smooth. Garnish with orange slices. Makes 2 servings.

HORSE'S NECK

Peel of 1 lemon, cut in a spiral

Ice cubes

Ginger ale

Place lemon peel in glass; dangle end over rim. Fill glass with ice cubes; then fill with ginger ale. Makes 1 serving.

GREEN GRAPE GLACIER

12 seedless green grapes

½ cup white grape juice

½ cup cold sparkling water

Freeze grapes until hard. Combine 10 frozen grapes and grape juice in a blender and process about 20 seconds or until smooth and thick. Pour into glass and add sparkling water. Stir gently. Garnish with remaining 2 frozen grapes. Makes 1 serving.

GRAPEFRUIT HONEY

1 sugar cube

2 dashes bitters

1 (2-inch-long) lemon twist

Ice cubes

Cold sparkling water

Put sugar cube in glass and splash with bitters. Add lemon twist; fill glass with ice cubes. Add sparkling water to fill. Makes 1 serving.

LEFT TO RIGHT: HORSE'S NECK, GRAPEFRUIT HONEY, GREEN APPLE COCKTAIL, GREEN GRAPE GLACIER, GRENADINE RICKEY

KIWI COOLER

1 ripe kiwifruit, peeled and sliced

2 tablespoons cream of coconut

2 tablespoons lime juice

¾ cup cold sparkling water

Reserve 1 kiwifruit slice. Combine remaining kiwifruit, cream of coconut and lime juice in a blender. Process about 10 seconds or until smooth. Pour into glass. Add sparkling water; stir. Garnish with reserved kiwifruit slice. Makes 1 serving.

LIME FROTH

⅔ cup lime juice

¼ cup sugar

2 egg whites

1 cup crushed ice

Lime slices

Combine lime juice, sugar, egg whites and crushed ice in a blender. Process about 20 seconds or until frothy. Garnish with lime slices. Makes 2 servings.

MOONLIGHT SERENADE

2 tablespoons apple brandy

2 teaspoons lemon juice

2 teaspoons Grenadine syrup

Ice cubes

2 peach slices

¾ cup cold sparkling water

Combine apple brandy, lemon juice and Grenadine syrup in a cocktail shaker with ice cubes. Shake well; strain into glass. Add peach slices and sparkling water; stir gently. Makes 1 serving.

MELON QUENCHER

1 cup seedless green grapes

1 cup white grape juice

1 cup ripe honeydew cubes

Reserve 4 grapes. Combine remaining grapes, grape juice and honeydew in a blender. Process about 15 seconds or until smooth. Garnish each serving with 2 of the reserved grapes. Makes 2 servings.

MINT JULEP

10 fresh mint leaves

2 teaspoons powdered sugar

2 teaspoons peach syrup

Ice cubes

1 cup cold sparkling water

Mint sprig

Combine mint leaves and powdered sugar in bottom of glass. Crush together with a spoon. Add peach syrup, then fill glass with ice cubes. Add sparkling water; stir gently. Garnish with mint sprig. Makes 1 serving.

MIXED DOUBLES

6 tablespoons lemon juice

¼ cup lime juice

2 tablespoons honey

Ice cubes

1½ cups cold sparkling water

Lemon slices

Lime slices

Combine lemon juice, lime juice and honey in a small pitcher. Stir well. Fill pitcher with ice cubes. Add sparkling water; stir gently. Garnish with lemon slices and lime slices. Makes 2 servings.

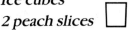

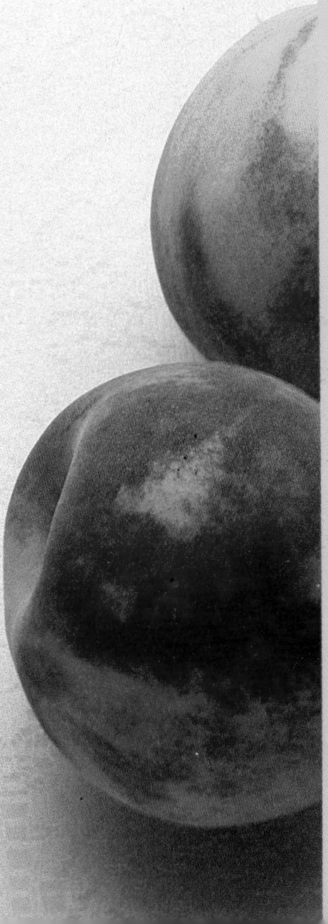

MINT JULEP

NELL GWYNN

Crushed ice

2 tablespoons apricot brandy

6 tablespoons orange juice

Orange slice

Fill glass with crushed ice. Add apricot brandy and orange juice. Stir gently. Garnish with orange slice. Makes 1 serving.

ORANGE HIGHBALL

Ice cubes

1½ teaspoons orange bitters

Ginger ale

Maraschino cherry

Orange slice

Fill glass with ice cubes. Add bitters. Fill glass with ginger ale; stir gently. Garnish with maraschino cherry and orange slice. Makes 1 serving.

PILGRIM'S PUNCH

Ice cubes

¼ cup grape juice

¼ cup cranberry juice

½ cup cold sparkling water

Lemon twist

Fill glass with ice cubes. Add grape juice, cranberry juice and sparkling water. Stir. Garnish with lemon twist. Makes 1 serving.

PILGRIM'S PUNCH

ORANGE SPRITZER

Crushed ice

2 tablespoons white grape juice

2 tablespoons Triple Sec or Cointreau

1 teaspoon lemon juice

6 tablespoons cold tonic water

Orange slice

Fill glass with crushed ice. Add grape juice, Triple Sec or Cointreau and lemon juice. Stir. Add tonic water; stir gently. Garnish with orange slice. Makes 1 serving.

PEAR ZINGER

2 tablespoons pear brandy or liqueur

1 teaspoon lemon juice

Ice cubes

½ cup ginger ale

Fresh strawberry, hulled

Combine pear brandy or liqueur and lemon juice in glass. Stir well. Fill glass with ice cubes. Add ginger ale; stir. Garnish with strawberry. Makes 1 serving.

ORANGE TRIPLEX

2 tablespoons frozen orange juice concentrate

1 tablespoon orange marmalade

1 teaspoon lemon juice

¼ teaspoon orange flower water

Cold sparkling water

Orange slice

Combine orange juice concentrate, marmalade, lemon juice and orange flower water in a blender. Process about 10 seconds or until smooth. Refrigerate until well chilled. Pour into glass, then fill glass with sparkling water; stir gently. Garnish with orange slice. Makes 1 serving.

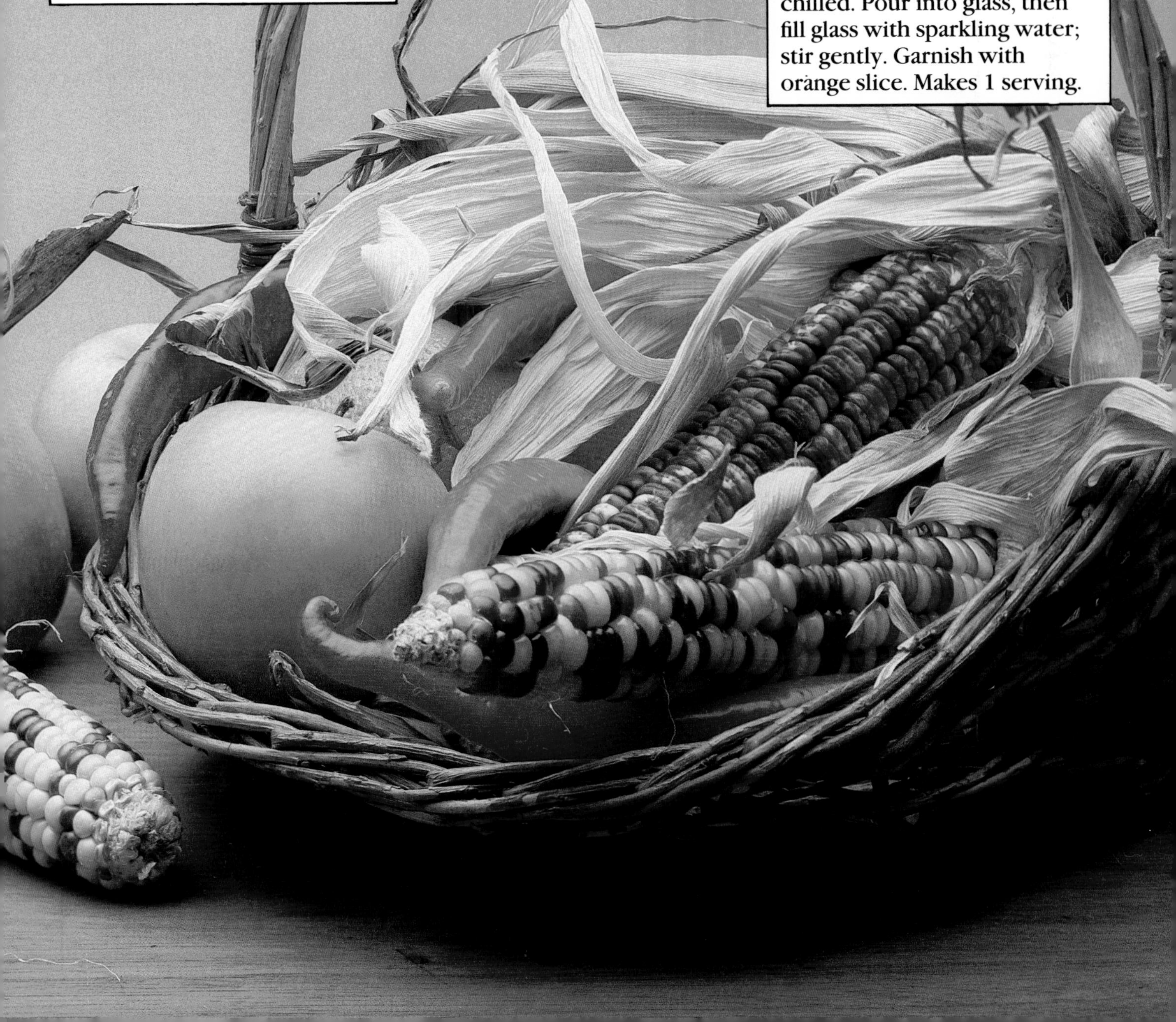

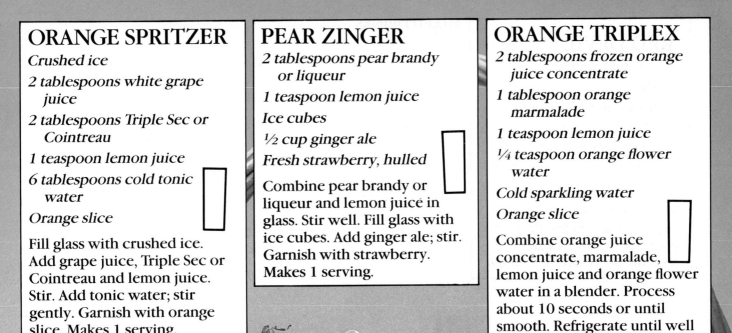

RED DEVIL

¾ cup tomato juice

1 egg

½ teaspoon hot-pepper sauce

Black pepper to taste

Ice cubes

Combine tomato juice, egg, hot-pepper sauce and black pepper in a blender. Process about 10 seconds or until smooth. Serve over ice cubes.

PIÑA COOLER

½ cup unsweetened pineapple juice

2 tablespoons cream of coconut

¼ cup unsweetened grapefruit juice

½ cup crushed ice

Pineapple spear

Maraschino cherry

Combine pineapple juice, cream of coconut, grapefruit juice and crushed ice in a blender. Process about 15 seconds or until creamy and thick. Garnish with pineapple spear and maraschino cherry. Makes 1 serving.

ROYAL FLUSH

Ice cubes

2 tablespoons cherry brandy

10 tablespoons ginger ale

Maraschino cherry

Fill glass with ice cubes. Add cherry brandy, then ginger ale. Stir gently. Garnish with maraschino cherry. Makes 1 serving.

ROYAL SWIZZLE

Ice cubes
½ cup cranberry juice
1 tablespoon lemon juice
Dash of bitters
½ cup ginger ale
Lemon slice
Orange slice

Fill glass with ice cubes. Add cranberry juice and lemon juice; stir. Add bitters and ginger ale; stir gently. Garnish with lemon slice and orange slice. Serve with a straw. Makes 1 serving.

LEFT TO RIGHT: ROYAL FLUSH, PUSSYFOOT, RED DEVIL, PIÑA COOLER, ROYAL SWIZZLE

PUSSYFOOT

1 tablespoon lemon juice
2 tablespoons lime juice
6 tablespoons orange juice
2 teaspoons powdered sugar
1 egg yolk
Crushed ice
6 tablespoons cold sparkling water
Orange slice

Combine lemon juice, lime juice, orange juice, powdered sugar and egg yolk in a cocktail shaker. Add crushed ice and shake well. Strain into glass. Fill glass with sparkling water; stir gently. Garnish with orange slice. Makes 1 serving.

SHIRLEY TEMPLE

1 tablespoon Grenadine syrup

10 tablespoons ginger ale

Maraschino cherry

Put Grenadine syrup in glass. Add ginger ale; stir gently. Garnish with maraschino cherry. Makes 1 serving.

SOURBALL

Ice cubes

2 tablespoons apricot brandy

2 tablespoons lemon juice

6 tablespoons orange juice

Maraschino cherry

Fill glass with ice cubes. Add apricot brandy. Add lemon juice and orange juice; stir gently. Garnish with maraschino cherry. Makes 1 serving.

SUNDOWNER

1 cup white grape juice

¾ cup cold sparkling water

Ice cubes

Mint sprigs

Combine grape juice and sparkling water in a small pitcher. Serve over ice cubes; garnish with mint sprigs. Makes 2 servings.

TROPIQUE

Ice cubes

2 tablespoons banana-flavored liqueur

½ cup unsweetened grapefruit juice

1 (1-inch) banana slice

Fill glass with ice cubes. Add liqueur and grapefruit juice. Stir. Garnish with banana slice. Makes 1 serving.

VIRGIN MARY

6 tablespoons tomato juice

2 teaspoons lemon juice

Dash of hot-pepper sauce

Dash of Worcestershire sauce

Black pepper to taste

Ice cubes

Small celery stalk with leaves

Combine tomato juice, lemon juice, hot-pepper sauce, Worcestershire sauce and black pepper in a cocktail shaker. Shake well with ice cubes. Strain into glass. Garnish with celery stalk. Makes 1 serving.

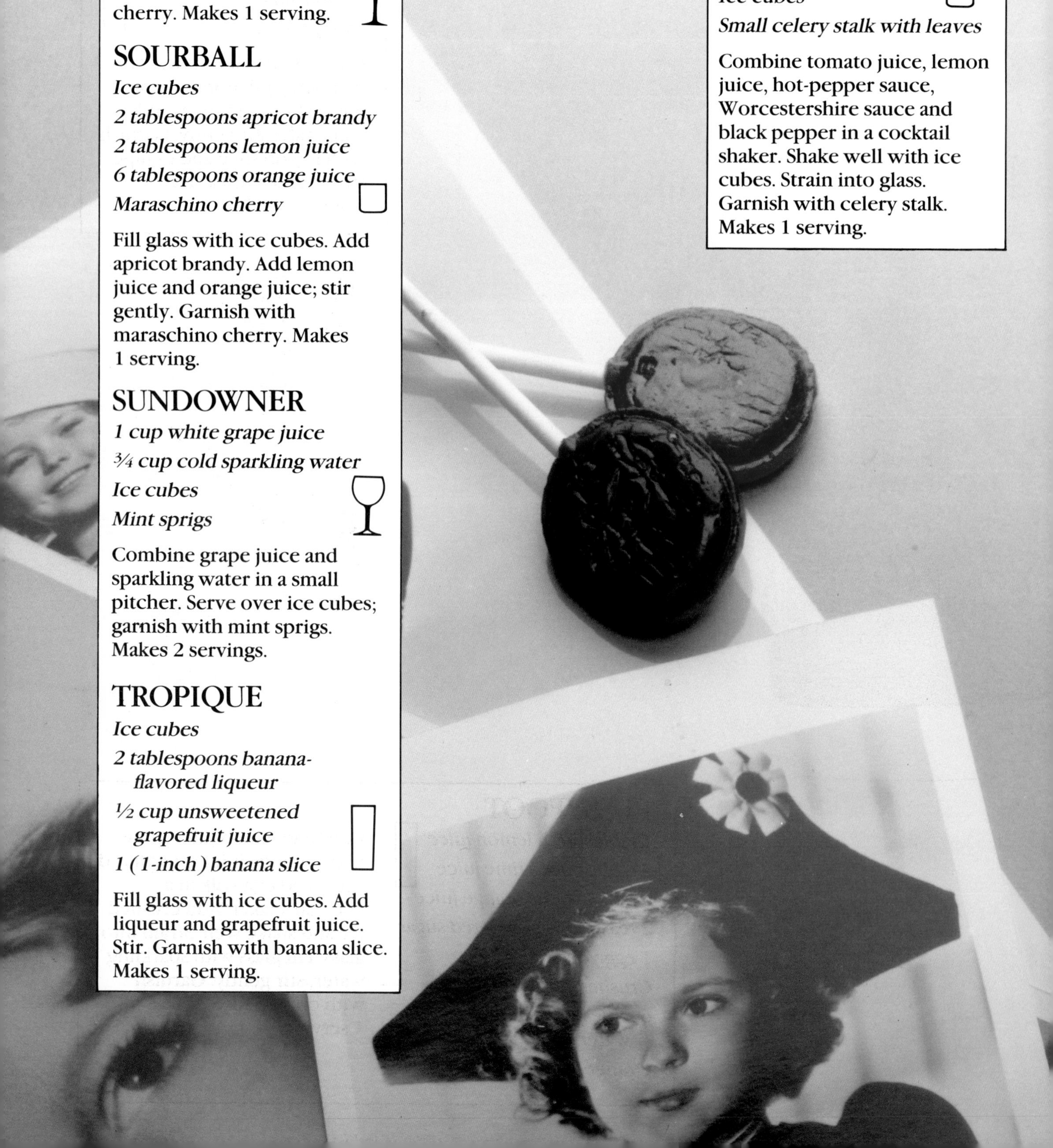

YOGI

2 tablespoons plain yogurt
¾ cup bitter-lemon soda
Ice cubes

Combine yogurt and ¼ cup bitter-lemon soda in glass. Stir until well blended. Fill glass with ice cubes and add remaining ½ cup soda. Stir gently. Makes 1 serving.

SHIRLEY TEMPLE

Index

Special thanks to The Pottery Barn Inc.

All photography by Edward Hing and Janine Norton.

Photo Credits
Glassware pages 6, 8, 10–11 (except fourth from left), 20–21, 24–25, 26–27, 30–31, 36–37, 39, 40, 46, 48, 49 (right), 50, 53, 58, 60, 62–63, 71, 72–73, 76, 78–79, 80–81, 88, 92, 94–95. 97, 98–99, 110–111, 118, 120–121, 124, 126–127, 128, 132–133, 136–137, 138, 140–141, 142, 145, 146–147, 150–151 and 152–153 courtesy The Pottery Barn Inc.; baskets pages 29, 39 and 143, bowl page 52, tea infusers pages 58–59, milk pitcher page 86 also courtesy The Pottery Barn Inc.

Espresso Plus electric espresso maker pages 8 and 77, Biomaster juicer page 42, coffee grinder page 76, Brewmaster coffee-maker page 77 courtesy Krups.

"Osterizer" blender pages 13 and 138 compliments of Oster Co., Milwaukee, WI.